CLASSROOM TIME MANAGEMENT

BOOK II: ORGANIZING STUDENTS

Revised Edition

Dick Webster
Dave Bailey

Webley Associates, Rochester, Minnesota 55902

The editors were Dr. E. Gershon, Warren Zimmerman, and Darla Olson.
The cover was designed by Doug Case and his high school students.
Modern Press was the printer and binder.
Published by:

Webley Associates
937-7th Avenue S.W.
Rochester, MN 55902
(507) 288-8074
If no answer, call (507) 282-7834

CLASSROOM TIME MANAGEMENT

Book II: Organizing Students

ISBN 1-881449-01-7

ABOUT
THE AUTHORS

Dick Webster is presently a retired Staff Development Coordinator, K-12, from the Rochester Independent School District 535. Currently, he is on the adjunct staff for Winona State University, teaching graduate classes on "The Improvement of Instruction. "He taught physical education Pre-K through high school, directed health and physical education programs K-6 for 16 years, coordinated athletic programs K-12, and was the director of the Winona State University Graduate Induction Program for three years.

Dave Bailey is presently a Clinical Supervisor for the Winona State University Graduate Induction Program K-6. He has supervised over 30 student teachers and taught grades 6, 5, and 3. He was one of the eleven selected for the Minnesota Education Association's 1991 Teachers of Excellence. In addition, he has taught numerous staff development and college classes in the areas of Peer Coaching, Cooperative Learning, and Time Management.

BOOK II   Organization Students

CLASSROOM TIME MANAGEMENT

Book I Organizing Self and Others

Book II Organizing Students

Book III Organizing Work

NOTE TO TEACHERS

This book is made up of many ideas which are effective to different styles of teaching. The same skill or activity may be done in a number of different ways and still be time-efficient and effective for a teacher.

The real purpose of this book is to share some of the time-efficient and effective ideas of teachers so that other teachers can use them, modify them, or brainstorm other ideas from the ones given; in order to develop better classroom time management.

There are not enough hours in the day to do all the things that <u>could</u> <u>be</u> <u>done</u> in teaching, but maybe this book will help you be more time-efficient and effective with one or two of your current practices; so that in the end, this book will have been worthwhile to you.

THESE TIMESAVING IDEAS ARE BAR-CODED: **K-2** ON **TOP ONE THIRD,**

3-4 ON **MIDDLE THIRD**, and **5-6** on **BOTTOM THIRD OF EACH PAGE.** IDEAS

WHICH ARE ESPECIALLY APPLICABLE TO **ALL GRADES K-6** ARE **NOT BAR-**

CODED. PLEASE BE AWARE THAT MANY OF THE IDEAS SHARED BY

TEACHERS TRANSCEND ACROSS SEVERAL GRADE LEVELS. BE SURE TO

READ **ALL** THE GRADES' SUGGESTIONS IN ORDER TO PROFIT FROM THE

MANY OTHER EXCELLENT IDEAS.

Teachers described these timesaving ideas to us in detail. The ideas have been condensed purposefully to save your time. The main ideas are presented to you in a manner that should expedite your time. You may adapt them to your style and teaching situation.

It is our sincere wish that you will find several entries to save you time in many areas and make your profession the most enjoyable.

DEDICATION

We would like to dedicate this book to all the excellent teachers of Independent School District 535, Rochester, Minnesota, in remembrance of all their years of past, present, and future professional dedication.

From all the information received, there were three main themes that emerged over and over again from the majority of teachers interviewed. First, all of these teachers put many **extra** hours into their workday beyond the "required" time. Second, **planning**, both short- and long-range, was a very important part of their teaching schedule. Third, the use of students to do many of the daily tasks was developed through **direct teaching** of the **skills of independence** to students at grade levels K-6.

ACKNOWLEDGEMENTS

There were over one hundred teachers who made this book possible. The first group of teachers, who provided their expertise and ideas, are listed on the next page.

The second group of teachers, who shared their expertise and ideas, wished not to have their names listed.

The last group of teachers are those who were not asked to share their ideas due to time restrictions, but would have shared their ideas if asked.

A special "Thank You" to Warren Zimmerman, retired Elementary Principal, who assisted with the writing of the introductions to each chapter.

CLARIFICATION: Teachers were selected, by their grade levels (K-6), at each building, thus providing a mixture of teaching experiences.

Any errors in interpretations of the information given by teachers is unintentional.

TEACHERS CREDITED

Holly Anderson	Darlene Forbrook	Gloria Obermeyer
Joyce Anderson	Kathleen Freeberg	Herbert Ollenburg
Peggy Anderson	Bob Gray	Marlys Ostby
Sue Bock (Greenberg)	Bonnie Gunderson	Carol Passi
Ramona Back	Charles Healy	Bill O'Reilly
Bonnie Bailey	Diane Kinneberg	Linda Rud
Kim Benda	Kelly Kosidowski	Esther Schmidt
Bruce Bigelow	Jim Kulzer	Carol Schroedel
Barbara Campbell	Dorette Leimer	Phillip Settell
Janet Carstensen	Leo Loosbrock	Gwen Stanich
Rosemary Chafos	Scott Mahle	Joe Stanich
Jane Coy	Marilyn McKeehen	Bill Temple
Lois Crouch	Mary Beth Miller	Dorie Thamert
Betty Danielson	Nancy Mix	Tom Theismann
Char Davis	Evelyn Nauman	Arlene Thone
Joan Davis	Don Nelson	Lynn Tollar
Doris DeSart	Marilyn Norland	Jay VanOort
Tony Floyd		

Chapter I - Skills of Independence

INTRODUCTION

Independence is a behavior that is valued in the school setting and in the work place. It is important for students to develop skills of independence (or decision-making) so they can become more and more responsible for themselves in terms of behavior and learning.

It is not uncommon to hear this teacher statement, "My kids just don't listen!" Perhaps the reason for that statement is students have not been taught to listen. It cannot be <u>assumed</u> that students know intuitively how to do any number of skills that are necessary to function productively in the classroom.

Teaching skills of independence is a must. Why? According to Melinda Welsh:

1. "Students who can work independently can get additional practice on previous learning or can learn something new without the teacher's immediate presence."

2. "When students work independently, the teacher has uninterrupted time to meet with a group or an individual."

3. "Independence is a desirable characteristic throughout life."

STRATEGY

Assess the skills in terms of which are in place and working in the classroom and which need to be taught. Those in place and working should be maintained and reinforced. The rest should be taught as a content area would be, using lesson design format. If one or two students are lacking a skill, teach it individually or in a small group.

In doing a task analysis of the skill to be taught, the teacher must think of each objective needed to perform the skill and the information needed by the student in order to accomplish it. For example, if teaching the skill of responding to a signal, the learner must:

Objective for learner	The information needed to accomplish it
1. know the signal	1. "May I have your attention please?"
2. what to do when it is heard	2. - stop right away - look at teacher - keep looking until told to go back to work or to stop looking

It is understandable that individual teachers may have objectives and information tailored to their expectations or classroom format. The input step of the lesson design should accommodate the two-part planning.

INDEPENDENT LEARNER

Definition: An independent learner is a student able to make appropriate decisions and pursue tasks to completion without interrupting others. The student is accountable to answer for his/her own conduct and obligations without supervision.

This list can include any skills the teacher considers necessary for independence and additions are in order.

1. The student will react positively and quickly to the teacher's classroom signal.

2. The student will be able to move within the classroom appropriately as follows:

   a. goes to appropriate space to work
   b. moves about the room without disrupting others
   c. takes care of personal needs according to the classroom procedures (drinks, rest room, breaks, sharpens pencils, etc.)

3. The student will be able to be responsible for his/her own self-improvement as follows:

   a. knows that the first step in self-improvement is liking yourself
   b. knows that he/she and others deserve only appropriate behavior
      - verbal
      - non-verbal
      - touch

c. defines self-improvement: taking action to make ourselves better in some way

d. states three aspects of self-improvement:
- It is a need.
- It helps us feel good about ourselves.
- It is a potential in everyone.

e. identifies the "thought-action-feeling" circle as follows:
- Positive thoughts lead to positive feelings which encourage positive thoughts.

f. knows that self-improvement positively affects his/her self-concept

4. The student will be able to use material (supplies/equipment) appropriately as follows:
   a. gets the materials needed for the task
   b. conserves materials (uses only what is needed)
   c. uses materials so they may be satisfactorily used again by others
   d. returns materials to the correct location in an appropriate way

5. The student will be able to perform optional/required tasks at the appropriate ability level effectively and efficiently as follows:
   a. follows the prescribed procedures (rules, safety, and directions)
   b. works continuously without allowing self to be unnecessarily distracted
   c. begins within an acceptable period of time
   d. returns to the task after an interruption without undue delay
   e. completes task according to appropriate criteria
   f. records any data needed at the completion of a task
   g. budgets time; i.e., matches task, time available, and teacher expectations
   h. uses resources available for assistance in an appropriate way
   i. knows what to do when stuck (needs help)

6. The student will be able to identify and deal with his/her feelings in an appropriate manner as follows:
   a. recognizes that:
      - feelings are just feelings, not good or bad
      - everyone has the same feelings
   b. distinguishes different types of behavior that feel good (nurturing) to self and others
      - verbal ("I like you." "Thank you.")
      - nonverbal (a smile)
      - touch (hugs, kisses, shoulder rubs, and touch to the arm/shoulder)

"There are no shortcuts to any place worth going."

--Beverly Sills

c. knows that everyone has feelings and feelings can be managed
These feelings include the following:
- anger   - loneliness
- worry   - discouragement
- jealously   - confusion
- pride   - embarrassment
- love   - fear

d. demonstrates ways of expressing feelings and the effects on self and others by:
- decrease on "stuffing," and negative to self and others
  - emphasis on positive to self and others

e. demonstrates sharing of feelings

f. examines and trusts his/her own feelings

g. expresses and shows empathy to others

7. The student will be able to be responsible for his/her own behavior as follows:

a. demonstrates what to do if he/she experiences anyone who bothers, scares, or touches him/her in a way that he/she does not like
- say "NO"
- get away
- tell someone right away

b. explains/demonstrates appropriate ways to refuse to participate in behavior he/she is confused/uncomfortable with
- verbal
- nonverbal
- touch

c. by saying "NO" to others if he/she is asked to do something which is wrong or feels wrong, unacceptable behavior
- physical abuse
- mental abuse
- sexual abuse

d. demonstrates that he/she is responsible for his/her own behavior and not for the behavior of others
- verbal
- nonverbal
- touch

e. explains the controllable and uncontrollable factors in his/her life as follows:
- controllable choices/behavior (How I treat myself, how I treat others, and how I treat property/environment)
- uncontrollable factors - non-choices (race/color, heredity factors, and situations)

4

8. The student will interact appropriately with the environment in the following ways:
   a. appropriate language
   b. sharing
   c. cooperation
   d. without physical aggression

9. The student will be able to know which of the following support systems he/she has to seek for help:
   a. goes to appropriate sources for help (materials, peers, others)
   b. determines who he/she can tell if he/she experiences an uncomfortable or bad behavior
       - mom/dad, guardian
       - teacher
       - principal
       - friend
       - neighbor
       - school nurse
       - school social worker
       - policeman
       - school crossing guard
       - clergy
       - school secretary
       - school counselor

10. The student will be able to make choices when available.
    a. can identify choices available
    b. can state purpose for each activity
    c. can match own needs (instructional) with appropriate activity
    d. makes an appropriate choice of activity when the opportunity exists

RESOURCES

Based on Interpersonal Relations Elementary Classroom Teacher Guide, Touch Continuum K-6, Jefferson's "Positive Action" Program, Kindergarten Intervention Program, UCLA Independent Learner (Lab School: Dr. Hunter, and "Classroom Management Instructional Training Workshop.")

Introduction and skill list taken from ISD 535 Staff Development Handbook (1987), pages 187, 190, 270-273.

NOTES:

"If you burn out, you most likely are doing too much for the students versus them doing it."

--Joe Stanich

SKILLS OF INDEPENDENCE

SELF-DIRECTED LEARNING Schedule a 15 minute period each day as a self-directed learning time. Students get choices of activities of homework, review, make-up work, or reinforcement. Ideas include water painting, library book reading, activity booklets, art scrap drawer, reading games, puzzles, math manipulatives, your choice . . . .

ANSWER OWN PROBLEMS I teach students to answer own problems first before seeing me. They look to self first and then to another student **before** coming to me.

STUDENT ORGANIZATION Make sure students are better organized than I am to help save me time. It takes more time initially but saves time the rest of the school year.

STUDENT INDEPENDENCE When students start to schedule their own time and develop a sense of independence for selections of related activities for curriculum extension, based upon assignments, list on the chalkboard. It takes a lot of effort and time to develop this and refine it, but it really saves a large amount of time all year long and students are more at their own level of difficulty.

"Students do about everything children are responsible for if you allow them to."

--Carol Schroedel

LESSON DESIGN - Skills of Independence Stations

Anticipatory Set: I show the students the box of cards that list the activities for the stations. As I read the cards I show the students the materials for each station.

Objective: I tell the students these are activities that they may do alone or with someone when their work for the day is completed. I also explain that each station has certain directions that need to be followed to complete the task and the reason why this is important to the student.

Input: I take 2 - 3 activities each day and discuss how and why they are to do each activity. We discuss 2 - 3 activities each day until all have been explained. We also review the previous activities in order that the students may hear the directions more than 1 time.

Modeling: I show the students how to do each activity. I might demonstrate the activity or actually do the activity with the students.

Check for Understanding: At the end of each demonstration of an activity I would ask students to repeat the directions for each activity.

Guided Practice: I do the activities that are most difficult in small groups and help with the directions until all can do the activities independently.

Independent Practice: Students participate alone or in small groups, in station activities when they have completed their assigned work for the day.

Closure: Review activities and why students are participating in these activities. Also remind students that learning takes place in many ways, direct instruction, independent work, and small groups.

Lesson Plan by Mary Reagan. October, 1989.

S.T.E.P.S.
Students Trying Effective Practice Skills to Independence

Anticipatory Set -

Do I know what to do?
Do I have the materials?
Can I answer my own questions?
Can I ask a friend?
Last of all check with the teacher.

Objective -

To teach specific steps in independent learning. The reason this is important is that each of you will be able to be more independent, thereby saving you time and becoming more productive.

Input -
Discuss the assignment board and what is expected of students.

Modeling -
Do an assignment with the class from the ones listed on the assignment board. Show where the Teacher's Manual and Answer Keys will be placed for self correcting.

Check for Understanding -
Walk around the room to monitor progress and answer questions.

Guided Practice -
Check each student on a specific task.

Independent Practice -
Refer students to the original questions in Anticipatory Set.

Closure -
Discuss the task accomplished and the advantages of being a self-actualized learner.

S.T.E.P.S. by Katie Gibson, October, 1989.

SKILLS OF INDEPENDENCE
by Andrea Johnson

Half of our building has open classrooms. FOURTH and FIFTH grades are housed here. When the students become FOURTH GRADERS, they must learn a new, more disciplined, hallway behavior.

1. ANTICIPATORY SET

"Everyone turn around and look into the hallway area. What do you see? What do you think it would be like if we had no rules about hallway behavior in this building?" Brainstorm what would happen if there were no rules; brainstorm ideas.

2. OBJECTIVES

"You will learn the correct and quiet way to walk through our building. We can't disturb other classrooms, just like we don't want other classes to disturb us.

3. INPUT

Explain how the class is to line up in two lines. The line leaders are in front. All face forward with no talking.

4. MODELING

The teacher goes out into the hallway and stands where the line leader will stand -- next to coat locker. Teacher faces forward, not talking.

5. CHECKING FOR UNDERSTANDING

Call on some students to explain why we need to have a quiet line in hallways and to explain how they are to line up.

6. GUIDED PRACTICE

Line leaders line up.
Rows 1-3 line up.
Rows 4-6 line up.
Check that all students are facing forward and not talking. Take a walk down the hall.

7. INDEPENDENT PRACTICE

Each time children, as a whole class or in small groups, leave the classroom, they are to line up and practice the correct hallway behavior.

8. CLOSURE

"Did the class do a good job in the hallways today?"

Independence, Lesson Design, Desk Maps (organization of desk)

I. Anticipatory Set

Option "A" - Role Play.....using two students (1 student whose desk is neat and organized; 1 student whose desk is disorganized). Teacher tells both that the principal is waiting for both of them in her office (positive reward - these two students bring their book down to her and read orally to her).

The student who has a neat desk immediately finds book in desk and heads down to the office. The student who has a disorganized desk keeps searching for book but can't find it. He/she finally finds it, but it's too late-- the principal left for a meeting.

Discussion would follow.

Option "B" - Pretend. Explain to students that their class was chosen to be in a group contest at the State Fair for organization of desks. Rules: Each student must have an organized desk (criteria taught by teacher). Surprise visits by a judge will occur during the year (six visits minimum). The desks will be evaluated each time--a score is given to the group each time. Scores are tabulated to see if class will be entered in the State Fair.

Discussion.

II. Objective

Students will be able to independently organize his/her desk according to his/her desk map.

Objective will be orally stated, written on the overhead, and written on a poster board to be kept.

III. Input

Discuss organization (definition - in dictionary) and application.

Do short brainstorming session related to the advantages/disadvantages of having an organized versus a disorganized desk. Discussion related to the advantages of having an organized desk. (Emphasis)

Explain to students that they will be learning a new method of organizing the inside of their desks using a desk map. (Emphasize independence)

Explain all steps of desk map.

IV. Modeling

Show desk maps again **(see example "A", p. 13)** on paper in front of class. Hand out a copy to each student. Show transparency on overhead. Teacher models the expected outcome with an empty desk. While teacher does the desk, he/she puts in one book, notebook, etc. at a time.

One student is selected to "model" the behavior with the teacher (partners: teacher + student).

V. Checking for Understanding

To check students' understanding, each student uses his/her own "chalkboards" (chalkboards are in a zip lock plastic bag, along with chalk and an old rag or sock to erase things).

Each student is asked to write down (in correct sequence) the order of items found on the desk map. What items go where.

Student holds up chalkboard to check if student understands concept.

VI. Guided Practice

Cooperative partner work--two people work as partners and actually set up a "pretend" desk on top of their desk. Each set of partners is responsible for setting up their materials correctly. (Only one desk is done.) Teacher checks for accuracy of each desk.

VII. Independent Practice

Students are responsible for setting up their own inside of desk. They tape their desk maps to the top inside of their desk for quick review throughout the year.

After student is done, teacher checks individual desks - positive reinforcement given if applicable.

VIII. Closure

Closure A: (Refers to Anticipatory Set "A")
Role play two students (organized desk). See if both students would be able to find book so they can read to principal.

Closure B: (Refers to Anticipatory Set "B")
Review the State Fair (pretend rules). Remind the students that a judge will be in a minimum of six times to check their desks.
Emphasize group goal for independence and State Fair challenge.

DESK MAP

BOOKS

SCIENCE
SOCIAL STUDIES WORKBOOK
SOCIAL STUDIES
READING WORKBOOK
READER
HANDWRITING
SPELLING
ENGLISH
MATH

LONG TERM
PROJECTS

NOTEBOOKS
NOTEBOOK PAPER
LIBRARY BOOKS
THINGS TO GO
HOME

WRITING +
ART TOOLS
TOKENS
NAME TAGS

PENCIL BOX

TISSUES

ALWAYS PUT USED BOOKS AT BOTTOM OF PILE.
ONLY PUT ITEMS TO TAKE HOME ON TOP OF RIGHT PILE
STORE ALL WRITING + ART TOOLS, TOKENS, AND NAME TAGS
IN PENCIL BOX.

NOTES:

"Students are responsible for themselves. Expect a lot and you get a lot."

--LaVonne Ryberg (1989)
A Rochester Teacher

Chapter II - Routines

TEACHER PLEASE NOTE: Please be aware that many of the ideas shared by teachers can and do transcend across several grade levels. Be sure to read all grades' suggestions in order to profit from the many other excellent ideas.

INTRODUCTION

Routines must be taught. Don't assume anything. Our procedures seem like "old hat" to us. New students have no basis of understanding them without instruction.

Time will be well invested in this area. Routines provide quicker transitions between areas, reduce disruptions, maintain lesson flow and set a positive room atmosphere. All this adds up to gaining time for instruction.

Don't forget to address flexibility. Being <u>too</u> rigid or not changing things once in a while can result in boredom.

During a real disaster, such as a fire drill, you won't be able to go back to reteach a routine. Do them right the first time. <u>Routines are only as important as the time and effort YOU put into them</u>.

One third of the first week of school should be spent on teaching routines. Establish ideas for handling the suggestions that follow. The list is not inclusive. You may think of other ideas as you are reading through them.

"Time is very dangerous without a rigid routine. If you do the same thing every day at the same time for the same length of time, you'll save yourself many a sink. Routine is a condition of survival."

Flannery O'Connor
1925-1964

ROUTINES

The following are areas of <u>Routines</u> that have been suggested by grade levels K-6. Choose those that apply to your style, class, school, and grade level. As you think about these specific areas, it may also remind you of other classroom procedures you may need.

lunch count
tardy/absent/attendance procedures
understanding of daily/weekly schedule
arrival procedure
dismissal procedure
beginning and ending of day routine
coat hooks/lockers
lining up
movement to special areas/teachers
traffic patterns
break/snack/lunchtime routines
noon hour indoor/outdoor
playground safety
    - phy. ed. shoes/dress
    - equipment
    - sidewalks
    - parking areas
    - entrances
building safety
    - classroom
    - hallway
    - lunchroom
    - restrooms
    - auditorium (gym)
bus safety
field trip expectations
fire and disaster drills
teacher out of the room
school patrol
medications
illness/first aid
permission slips
transition to subject areas
collecting assignments
distributing materials/equipment
getting materials/equipment
use of materials/equipment
care of materials/equipment
art work
drinks
games
free time out

format for assignments/paper/
    headings
quality of work
speaking/voice levels
consideration of others
study versus work times
out-of-seat policies
student attention during
    presentations
talk among students
student participation
obtaining help
classroom helpers
behavior during interruptions
signals
phone/intercom use
use of teacher's desk/materials
use of students' desks
use of storage areas
choices (if finished early)
use of learning centers/stations
cooperative learning group
    behavior
birthdays
manuscript or cursive writing
pen or pencil
late work
incomplete work
coloring/drawing on papers
keeping track of assignments
how to display work
written comments on work
correcting papers
personal spelling list
parent communication:
    - newsletters, phone calls,
    - written notes
bathroom procedures
correcting papers
sharpening pencils
homework
wastebasket

PERSONAL SPACE	At the beginning of the school year, put X's on the carpeted floor with masking tape to insure enough personal space when you ask them to come and sit down next to you. After they learn where to sit, remove the X's from the floor.
MARK AREAS	Put plastic tape on the floor or carpet to mark certain areas: walk ways, spots to sit for show and tell, and areas to line up at.
SEPARATE SPACES	If you have several classes in the same area for an assembly, or a special area teacher, put tape on the floor to separate the space into areas for each class. This organization makes it easier to dismiss and everyone knows where to sit ahead of time, for faster starts.
REGULAR LAVATORY BREAKS	Set regular times for lavatory breaks during the day. Most students should be able to wait until one of them arrives. Before and after recess, phy. ed., and lunch are natural times.
SELF-DIRECTED LAVATORY BREAKS	A self-directed lavatory design, that allows the teacher to see at a glance who is out, can be accomplished with notecards. Put each student's name on 3 x 5 notecards and laminate them. Punch a hole in each. Simply have the student hang his/her name on the appropriate Boy or Girl nail by the door as they leave. One at a time, of course.
LAVATORY PASSES	Make up two brightly colored, permanent lavatory passes. One for girls and one for boys. Cover them with clear contact paper for durability. Anytime a student needs one, they just take it off your desk and put in on top of theirs. You can quickly check if a student is out of the room (look at your desk) and can tell who is gone by looking at their desks.
SIGNAL LAVATORY BREAKS	For better control of lavatory breaks, teach the children to come up to you and hold their hand up near your shoulder. Just a nod of your head yes or no will give them the next direction. It teaches the younger child responsibility and allows you to keep a tight handle on where the children are.
USE OF LARGE LETTER PASSES	Purchase large wood or plastic colored letters of **B**, **G**, and **L**. They stand for **B**oys, **G**irls, and **L**ibrary. When a student goes to the **B**oy's Lavatory, **G**irl's Lavatory, or the **L**ibrary, they get the letter from my desk and put it on their desk. One quick look will tell you who has gone where.

**TIME
DRINKS**

When the total class is getting drinks at the fountain, assign one student to be a counter: "1 and 2 and 3 and 4 and 5-- STOP." An easy tap on the student's arm tells him/her it's time to take their seat or go to the end of the line if they're still thirsty. This cuts down on break time after phy. ed., recess, and lunchtime.

**MAGNETIC
OBJECT**

Try using magnetic objects for indicating students who have left the room. The student puts the magnetic object on the front of his/her metal desk and you can see at a glance who is out of the room and for what purpose.

**STUDENT
NUMBER**

Use the assigned student numbers for textbook identification, paper work handed in, locker assignments, and to reinforce math concepts. Line up by odd or even numbers, in order, in reverse order, by sets, by 2's, by 5's, patterns, etc.

GREETER

Assign a student to be **"greeter."** It is the student's job to answer the door, take messages, and to show visitors where to sit; students learn good manners by practicing them and you don't have as many interruptions.

**STUDENT
LEADER**

Assign a student to be **"student leader."** It is the student's job to answer other students' questions, correct papers, and call on students who raise their hands for a question while the teacher is working with a small group or is indisposed.

"Everything looks impossible for the people who never try anything."

Jean-Louis Etienne

ELIMINATE IN AND OUT OF ROOM	Make a rule: "If you come into the room, you must stay in the room." This cuts down on students running in and out of the room during lunch, break times, etc.
PAPERS TO BE TAKEN	Stack papers to be handed out next to the door. Students take one off of each pile as they come in the door in the morning or at noon. This saves time in passing out papers.
GYM SHOES	Have students put their gym (tennis) shoes on as they come into the room first thing in the morning. Valuable phy. ed. or classroom time will not be taken up.
WAIT TIME	Students need to know what to do while they wait for materials and directions. Establish a short list of appropriate behaviors or tasks to do. Think about noise level, body position, material placement on desks, pencil sharpened, or is their area neat?
AFTER COMPLETING WORK	When students are finished with their required work, suggest extra credit assignments, enrichment activities, free reading, learning centers, drawing, art work, or checking their assignment books.
TIME ON TASK	Allow drinks and pencil sharpening only during non-instructional time. You will find more on-task participation and not having to repeat so many directions.
SNACK BREAK	Don't waste time with snack breaks. Allow responsible students to take their snack break or even a short rest break on their own time as long as it is not disruptive to others. The classroom routine continues as usual.
PERMANENT PASSES	Make permanent passes for students to return to the classroom during noon hour. The teacher's name is written on a piece of formica and a hole drilled for yarn to be worn around the neck.
LAVATORY SIGN	Use a self-directed stop sign idea for lavatory permission: Have a large circle or figurine **(red on one side, for STOP, and green on the other, for OK)** for boys and another large circle or figurine for girls. When someone leaves, they turn their sign to red--no one else may leave. Upon their return they turn their sign back to green.

LAVATORY KEY

Use two key chains for the lavatory permission problem. Modeled after a filling station, the plan allows the student to pick up their Boy or Girl key chain when they leave and replace it when they return.

SIGN OUT

Have a **sign out** sheet for Boys/Girls. The student signs out their name and where they are going. They check off upon their return. This is a nice safety check for fire drills and when leaving the room as a class.

ROUTINE CHALLENGE

For making routines more fun, issue a challenge. Can you do such and such in _____ seconds? Keep records. Try to beat the records. Use an oven timer or stop watch.

LINE LEADERS

Have two **line leaders**. They lead two lines side-by-side so that the class doesn't stretch out so far. Instruct them to walk "slower than normal." They also are to STOP if they hear noise. The teacher walks at the end of the line to encourage the stragglers. It encourages responsibility and self-management.

PERSONAL SPELLING LIST

Have students make a **"Personal Spelling List"** on the back page of their spelling notebooks. Record all words they miss on tests and words they ask you how to spell during a six week period. This list then becomes their weekly test every six weeks. The departure from the regular units is refreshing, and they are studying the words THEY, personally, need to know. Partners give each other their tests. Use the personal spelling list as a key for correcting by stapling them together after the test is taken.

"There is nothing like a dream to create the future."

Victor Hugo

**START AND
END POSITIVE** Start and end each day on a positive note. Perhaps a quick discussion or review of the good things about the day. A positive feeling tone will do wonders for the teacher and the students.

**LEAVING
THE ROOM** Insist that students sit in their desks quietly before you leave to go to any other room or area in the building. This includes the first thing after the bell rings. This provides a change of pace and time to give directions, assignments, read the bulletin, take attendance, etc.

**NAMES ON
CHALKBOARD** Have students write their names on the chalkboard as they leave the room for the lavatory, etc. Then they erase it when they return. You can limit the number of names allowed out of the room at one time. It provides self-direction and allows you to know who is out.

**SIGN-OUT
SHEET** Use a student **sign-out sheet**. If a student leaves the room, he/she fills in the time left, destination, and time returned.

**OVERHEAD
MARKER** Divide a sheet of paper in half and cover it with contact paper. One side is labeled "Boys" and the other "Girls." As a student leaves the room, he/she write their name on the proper side with overhead marker. Their name is erased upon their return.

COOPERATION Establish the concept of working together (cooperation versus competition). Teach **how** to help each other. Use cooperative learning techniques. Hold cooperative class discussion for the purpose of group problem solving. Assign a different student leader each time to conduct the discussion. **(See example "A" and "A1", pp. 25-26)**

The address for Johnson and Johnson's cooperative learning manual, Circles of Learning, is

        Interaction Book Company
        7208 Cornelia Drive
        Edina, MN 55435

        (612) 831-9500

NOTES:

"*Whatever you want students to be able to do,*
TEACH NOT PREACH"

GREET YOUR STUDENTS

Greet students at the door each morning and have them say Hot or Cold, depending on which type of lunch they desire. Record only the typical smallest number (hot or cold) on a class list. When everyone is seated, check absentees and the rest should automatically be the other choice (hot or cold). Your roll taking and lunch slip should be filled out within 30 seconds after the bell rings. A business-like start sets the tone for the morning and saves you routinely calling off every student's name day after day.

SELF-DIRECTED LEARNING TIME

Schedule a 15-minute period each day as a self-directed learning time. Students get choices of activities of homework review , make-up work, or reinforcement. Ideas include water painting, library book reading, activity booklets, art scrap drawer, reading games, puzzles, math manipulatives, your choice...

ACTIVE PARTICIPATION

Ask for milk count, hot lunch count, etc. by having the students be active participants in standing up while you count. They will have to think about their choice and a fewer mistakes will be made when first learning this routine.

INVOLVE STUDENTS

Involve students in the planning of guidelines and routines. It will give them "ownership" and mean more than those imposed upon them without input.

BASIC RULES

Choose 3 to 5 basic rules for the classroom and teach them the first week of school. Post them for year-long review and focus. Ideas might include:

> Get assignments in on time
> Respect others
> Do your best
> Use good manners
> Safety is number one
> Work cooperatively
> Study period: No talking, <u>one</u> up at a time
> Work period: Quiet talking, two up at a time
> To teacher's desk by permission only

"Time is a river without banks."

Anonymous

HELPING EACH OTHER
Teach students to help each other. It gives them a chance to feel good by helping and establishes better peer relationships. Dependency upon the teacher is diminished with the "Ask a friend and then come back" to a request for help.

WEEKLY DESK CLEANING
Students should be expected to keep desks, tables, and student storage spaces clean and neat. Set aside a particular period of time each week for students to clean out desks. Straightening out materials is a good end-of-day routine to get into.

LIMIT NUMBER OF STUDENTS
Set up a rule that will not allow lines at the pencil sharpener, sink, drinking fountain, and lavatory. Limit the number at one time or call by rows that are ready to use these areas.

CONTROL TRAFFIC
Set up off-limit areas to students, such as teacher's desk and storage areas. Give them their own areas and material storage areas to use. This will keep the traffic pattern away from your area.

TRANSITION
Use movement within the room as a transitional method. This change of pace refocuses onto a new task and gives a much-needed physical stretch. Change areas, take a stretch break.

TEACH YOUR EXPECTATIONS
You **cannot** make assumptions about what students know or are able to do. One must assess and check out each desired behavior; then address areas of need by teaching or reteaching each routine that will be repeated the entire year. Let students know the exact expectation <u>and its purpose</u>.

STUDENT CHAIRS
Have students put their chairs up on top of their desks at the end of the day. Desk tops have to be cleaned first, and it speeds up the cleaning of the floor. Custodians like it better, too.

"If you're not part of the solution, you're part of the problem."

Anonymous

HOW DO YOU CHOOSE?

Activity Sheet

Name_____

We each have our own way of making a decision. But there are
certain steps all of us go through in doing so. Let's see what
they are.

Six Steps to Decision Making

Often we don't think about the way we decide things - the HOW of
choosing one thing or one action over another. Here's a
"problem" for you to solve so that you can think about the HOW of
decision making. Remember that usually when we solve problems,
there are many ways to solve them. The solution for possible
answers to steps 3, 4, 5 and 6 below.

Step 1

STATE THE PROBLEM:

_____

_____

Step 2

IDENTIFY THE ALTERNATIVES:

_____

_____

_____

Step 3

IDENTIFY THE CONSEQUENCES FOR EACH ALTERNATIVE:

Alternative_____

    Good Consequence_____

    _____

    Bad Consequence_____

    _____

Alternative_____

    Good Consequence_____

    _____

    Bad Consequence_____

    _____

Alternative_____

    Good Consequence_____

    _____

    Bad Consequence_____

    _____

Step 4

WHAT'S IMPORTANT TO ME?

_____

_____

Step 5

MAKE A DECISION:

_____

_____

AM I HAPPY WITH MY DECISION? _____

Step 6

    WHY?_____

Chapter III - Signals

INTRODUCTION

Implement procedures for consistent signaling by reinforcing good compliance and periodic review. Perhaps put a reminder in your Lesson Plan Book once a month to address them.

Purposeful signals are needed for such things as noise level, readiness for instruction, listening for directions, listening for an announcement, or a prerequisite for something special.

Preplanned signals should provide a solid time saver throughout the school year. If one signal doesn't work, drop it and give another one a trial test for awhile.

This chapter will address the use of verbal and nonverbal signals.

SIGNALS for K-6

The following are signal ideas that have been suggested by grade levels K-6. Choose those that apply to your style, class, and grade level.

VERBAL/AUDITORY

signal words like **"freeze"** or **"buzz"** "May I have your attention," etc.
short verbal directions   "On the count of _____, be ready,"
whistle
count out loud
count in a different language
use a soft voice
use student names
snap of the fingers
clap of hands in a rhythm
a bell
a piano
a musical instrument

NONVERBAL/SILENT/VISUAL

count down on five fingers
an "OK" sign
index finger to your lips for silence
index finger motion to come up to you
thumb up or down
raise arm for silence
body placement in room
body language/facial expression/eye contact
model your wishes
point
use colored cards
a stare with good eye contact
use 2 fingers in a "V" for victory or the Cub Scout sign
switch lights off and on
stand in a specific place (like a podium or in front of the class)
turn on overhead projector
proximity control
physical touch

ANTICIPATE BEHAVIORS	Anticipate what students are going to do, plan ahead, and give verbal directions to stay out of trouble. For example, if you foresee anxious students getting ready for gym, bus, lunch, etc. say, "Stay in your chairs." Then you can give directions and excuse them orderly without having to get their attention all over again.
HALLWAY SIGNALS	When walking in the hallway, raise hand and hold five fingers up. If there is noise or other concern, drop a finger each few seconds. If all five are dropped, there should be a penalty.
REMINDERS	Point your finger at a student that needs a **"reminder"** that their behavior is unacceptable. After they see you, start raising your fingers, one at a time, if there is not an appropriate response right away. If you get to three, they are asked to leave the room. "Three strikes and you're out."
NOISE SIGNAL	An "OK" sign made with the thumb and index finger may be used to indicate "zero" noise, please.
INDIVIDUAL STUDENT SIGNAL	It is effective to use the index finger to motion a student to come to you and then whisper whatever is needed to be said to that child. This does not interrupt those already on task.
NONVERBAL SIGNALS	A nonverbal **"look"** tells students it's time to give you their complete, undivided attention. Facial expression that's sincere is "congruent" body language with your wishes.
SPECIAL PLACE SIGNAL	Walk over and sit in your **"special rocking chair."** This signals the students to quietly come over and sit down close to discuss a serious matter of importance. The other use of the chair is to regularly read to the class.
HEADS DOWN	Model by putting your own head down and folding your hands in front of you. Students are to follow suit. It gets distracting objects out of their hands, and voices stopped.
THUMBS DOWN	If a student approaches you at an inopportune time, just a thumbs down signal tells the student **"not now, sit back down."** No further explanation should be needed.
QUIET SIGNAL	An index finger to one's lips signals quiet without interrupting the whole class with a verbal signal. The **"shhhh"** just adds to the noise level, so leave that part out.

29

(Signals)

STUDENTS' SIGNALS

Students can signal visually to ask to go to the lavatory or sharpen a pencil. Non-auditory examples might be a thumb up for the bathroom and a pencil raised to ask permission to sharpen it. The teacher can then answer with a nod or shake of the head.

COLORED CARDS

Use three colored cards: Red, yellow, and green. Holding up a **red** means stop working, put things away; **yellow** equals a warning of not much time left; and **green** stands for start your work. **Yellow** may also stand for too much noise and **red** for "no talking."

VERBAL SIGNAL

A verbal signal of saying the work **"FREEZE"** stops the action quickly. Many times, this signal is also used in physical education, so the students are already conditioned to its use.

BREAK SIGNAL

When students have been working hard and you feel they could use a short break, have a signal such as a verbal **"Buzz."** They know that they can stop working and turn to someone near them and talk socially for 3-5 minutes. The signal to start back to work may be to just raise your hand in the air.

UNISON SIGNAL

When you wish to have a total class answer in unison, you can use the verbal signal **"anybody"** or a visual of cupping your hand behind your ear.

BEHAVIOR SIGNAL

A snap of the fingers is a strong reminder of proper behavior. It is especially effective while walking down the hallway, as it does not affect other classes by adding to the noise.

CONSISTENCY

A verbal **"pencils down; eyes up"** gives a quick, precise direction. If you use the same set of words consistently, they work better every time.

SET LIMITS

Be in control. Set your own limits dependent upon the activity. Say: **"On the count of _____ I want you to _____."** For example: **"On the count of 5 I want you to be seated in front of me with your eyes on me; then I'll know you're ready."**

COUNTING

Count 1, 2, 3, etc. in a normal voice and speed. This signals your desire for a change within the classroom. If 7 or 8 is reached before a change is forthcoming, a penalty is in order.

TIMER A concrete method of setting a timer to **"race against"** might get the job done. All must be in their seat and materials ready for the next subject before the bell rings.

BELL Ring a small bell to signal for attention. Don't overuse any signal. Keep this one for a **"special"** attention getter.

SING A SIGNAL Music is a natural attention getter. The teacher can sing a **"Clean Up"** song and insert names into the song along with directions to follow. Make up the words and melody as you go.

PIANO TUNE Play a tune or the scale on a piano. The students can sing along. It is a neat way to make a transition to the next subject. All the children are singing the same thing instead of having conversations.

CLAP A PATTERN Clap a musical pattern or beat. The children must echo it. Repeat it several times until everyone is with you and then you can start your next step. Vary the patterns for better auditory discrimination. An example is given below:

1/2	1/2	1/2	1/4	1/4	1/4
Ta	Ta	Ta	Tee	Tee	Tee
Long	Long	Long	Short	Short	Short

CLAP IN UNISON Raise your hand and then clap your hands. Repeat the same thing. Each time you should get additional students to clap with you at the same time in unison. When all students "have the beat," you are ready to begin. It gets their hands free of distracting objects at the same time.

POETRY CUBE Use a **"poetry cube."** Cover a small box (milk carton) with colored paper and put a poem on each side. Toss the box to a student and he/she reads the one facing up, while others say it along with them. A great sponge activity when switching to another activity.

31

BUS RIDE

Remember the game **"Little Red School House?"** A variation can be instead of the first person who talks is "out," limit the number of words each is allowed to say before they are "out." It works great on a short bus ride, and the challenge is like a game the children enjoy playing. Call it "Silence," and start with a maximum of 10 (your choice) words allowed. If they "lose," they can always play a 2nd, 3rd, ...round.

SPECIAL CHAIR

If you have a **"special chair"**, like a rocking chair, you can use it as a signal for serious discussions. Whenever you sit in it, the students are to come up and sit around you and be ready to discuss a problem,, decision, or anything especially serious.

*"If **telling** were the same as **teaching**, we would all be so smart we could hardly stand it."*

--Mark Twain

LIGHTS	Flick the room lights off for a visual, rather than a verbal, signal for the students to give you their attention. If you have two sets of switches, turn one back off as a two minute warning to stop and get ready for the next activity. When the light comes on, all should be ready to go.
OVERHEAD	A signal can be established for attention by turning on the overhead projector. Periodically, turn on the projector and start writing down names of students who are ready. You can give out stars which may be accumulated for prizes or to bid with on surprise auction bags.
THUMBS UP	A **thumbs-up** signal for quiet is a good visual signal. Students use the same signal if they are being disturbed by another student(s). It doesn't add to the noise level like an auditory signal does.
PROXIMITY	Proximity is an excellent nonverbal signal. Just stand by the student you want to get the message of calm down, pay attention, put distracting objects away, etc. Your close presence is many times all that is needed to affect a positive change in behavior. A touch on the shoulder can be added to this for emphasis.
YOUR HAND UP	Hold up your hand and **(the key)** the students hold up theirs, also. Be sure to hold out until 100% have hands up and are quiet with their eyes on you. Make it a race.
FRONT OF CLASS	Teach the children that whenever you walk to the front of the classroom, they are to stop what they are doing and look at you without talking. Your body placement is the nonverbal signal.
"V" SIGN	Raise two fingers in the air in a "V" configuration. It signals stop talking, look, and listen. Children who see you are encouraged to raise their hands to help signal quietly to others.
ANSWERS TRUE-FALSE	Students can signal answers by holding up fingers. One for "TRUE," two for "FALSE," an equal number of fingers for the syllables in a word, etc.

ASK FOR HELP

Do students shout out correct pronunciations or answers before a student has "think time" to figure it out themselves? Simply teach them the routine of unobtrusively raising their thumbs if they know the answer. **IF** the other students **want** help, they may call on the **"quietest"** thumb of their choice. The teacher may raise his/her thumb, too, of course. This works especially well in smaller groups like reading.

DIFFERENT LANGUAGE

To get ready for the next subject, count in a different language from 1 to 10. The students count with you. It gains attention, eliminates chatter, and is an educational sponge activity.

END OF LINE

When it is too noisy in the hallway, simply say, "If I can hear what you're saying, you're whispering too loud." If you can repeat what someone said, they have to go to the end of the line. If that doesn't solve the situation, impose a **NO TALKING** sanction until the next time you are in the hallway.

SOFTER VOICE

Voice level makes a difference. A **softer** voice promotes better listening. The students must strain to hear you. It makes it harder to talk and hear you at the same time.

WAIT TIME

A signal word followed by **"wait time"** is a pleasant way to get attention. Wait time with good eye contact is very effective.

INSTRUCTION TIME

A verbal signal of **"Pencils down; eyes up"** lets the children know you are ready and gives them instructions for listening at the same time. Repetitive use builds in the routine.

SIZE OF VOICE

Tell students what "size" voice is appropriate in certain situations. A **"six inch"** voice is a whisper near someone. A **"3 foot"** voice is talking to a friend nearby. It can go from **"zero"** to a **"room"** size voice.

"When schemes are laid in advance, it is surprising how often the circumstances fit in with them."

Sir William Osler

ATTENTION	Teach the children that if you turn on the overhead projector, full attention must be given quickly. Failure to do so may result in subtracting the same amount of time wasted from break time.
PODIUM	Teach the children that if you or a student is standing behind the podium, full attention must be given quickly. Failure to do so may result in subtracting a minute from break time.
INDIVIDUAL BASEBALL SIGNAL	An individual, preplanned **"baseball signal"** works great! The student should be talked to about this prior to use in the classroom. The student who needs to be reminded to be on task or regain control receives eye contact and a signal such as touching your nose, pulling your ear, or other simple cues.
PERSONALIZED SIGNAL	Set up personalized cue words or gestures for individual students. These reminders are only picked up on by the targeted student and show the student that you are especially concerned about him/her.
COUNTING	Count out loud after a visual signal is given for attention. If the class goes beyond a 3 to 5 (your choice) count, take away a point, or if they accomplish the goal, add a point. The tally goal can be celebrated with a perk on Friday.
STUDENT NAME	To redirect students in a positive way, use their name in a sentence to get their attention: "_____, **did you know that ------------?"**
TIME SAVED	Use a timer with consistent expectations. Any time saved is marked on the chalkboard and time over is subtracted. All the saved time over a period of a month becomes their party time.
LAST TIME	When the teacher or a student stands at the podium, charge the class lost time for not giving their full, quiet attention. Take it off break or free time.

NOTES:

"*You may delay, but time will not.*"

Ben Franklin
Poor Richard's Almanack
1748

MAKE-UP SIGNALS	Let the students make up their own signals to give to each other to hold noise level down to an acceptable level. Their creative natures come to the surface and the personal investment will make the ideas easier to remember and more fun to do.
CONSISTENT SIGNALS	If you're in a team situation or teaching multi-grade levels, establish the same signal(s) for consistency throughout. Coordination yields continuity and clearer communication. You won't have to take time to teach repetitive signals.
BUILDING CONSISTENCY	Find out what signals are used in the lunch room and physical education. Use appropriate ones in the classroom, also, since they are already familiar. Keep as much consistency as possible.
MULTI SENSORY INPUT	Give two signals at the same time. Some children respond better to one than the other. To stop the action, simply say **"Freeze"** and **raise your hand** at the same time. This provides an auditory and a visual clue. Students can be encouraged to raise their hands at the same time until it is quiet.
SPONGE ACTIVITY WITH ROUTINES	Use an audio tape as a sponge activity while you take attendance. Play examples of the "Composer of the Month," or something you have recently been studying.
TOUCH	Use proximity control and a light touch on the shoulder of a poor listener or disruptive student. This is a nonverbal signal which redirects attention.

NOTES:

"*Lost time is never found again.*"

Ben Franklin
Poor Richard's Almanack
1748

Chapter IV - Attendance and Lunch Count

TEACHER PLEASE NOTE:	Please be aware that many of the ideas shared by teachers can and do transcend across several grade levels. Be sure to read all grades' suggestions in order to profit from the many other excellent ideas.

INTRODUCTION

Can this mandatory duty be made more time efficient? Yes, it can. Read the suggestions taking place in classrooms today. Perhaps one of these is better suited than your current or past practice.

Five minutes off of this daily task computes to a savings of 2 1/2 <u>full</u> school days per year!

"Use more time to save time."

--Barb Campbell (1989)
A Rochester Teacher

NOTES:

"*I recommend you take care of the minutes:
for the hours will take care of themselves.*"

Lord Chesterfield
1694-1773

QUIET ASSIGNMENT
Have a quiet assignment to get started on right away in the morning. While students are having their self-directed study period, you have time to go around and take individual lunch count and interact with the students.

SMILIE CHART
Make a chart of smilie faces which students turn over as they come into the room. The smile greets them and signifies that they are present. Locate it near the doorway so it is not forgotten.

NAME TAGS
Give out name tags as the student arrives. Name tags left in the bucket must be absent. After the first few weeks of school, the students simply remove their name tag from one bucket and put it into another, eliminating the need to wear it. The bucket they put it into might be keyed into hot or cold lunch; or white or chocolate milk for break. Either way, the teacher need only count name tags in the appropriate bucket.

MILK COUNT
Paint clothespins white, brown, and leave some plain. Each morning the student chooses the color of milk by pinning the like-color clothespin next to their name on a tagboard class list. The plain clothespin signifies no milk. Take your attendance right off the chart.

LIBRARY CARDS
Have a bulletin board or tagboard poster with library card pockets, one for each child. Each student has four colored cards; **white** is turned up at the end of the day as they leave. As students come into the room at the start of the day they turn up a **yellow** to signify taking of cold lunch, **red** to signify eating out of the building with a parent, or **blue** to signify eating hot lunch at school. Just tape new names onto the library card pockets to get maximum use out of the display. Absentees are easily spotted as white cards left from the evening before.

TONGUE DEPRESSOR
Put each student's name on a tongue depressor. When they come into the room in the morning, they pick up their name and put into either the HOT or COLD can or pocket provided. A responsible student can very quickly mark in the attendance and hot lunch count for the day.

CLOTHESPINS Have each child's name on **both sides** of a clothespin. This makes them easier to find. When they come in the door, they find their clothespin and clip It to a cardboard triangle divided into three areas: Hot lunch, Cold lunch, and No lunch. A student can count up the number of clothespins in each section and even write the numbers in the correct columns on the attendance sheet.

SINGING Use music skills to take attendance. The teacher sings, "Where is __(student's name)__?" The child sings back, "Here I am," mimicking the same notes. Just go right down the class list or go randomly for better paying of attention.

PRACTICE TIME Use lunch count to practice with long and short vowel sounds. Students say a short "A" sound for hot lunch and a long "A" sound for cold lunch. Vary this to your current curriculum.

COUNT OFF Have younger students count off for HOT or COLD lunch. You get an accurate count for the office while the sponge activity has helped youngsters learn their numbers and shown them a practical application for them.

SPONGE ACTIVITY A great sponge math activity is to tell them the hot lunch count and instruct them to figure out how many cold lunchers there are by knowing the total class number minus any absentees. Then check their answers by counting the number of cold lunchers. It is a thinking skills activity, as well.

NUMBER SKILLS Reinforce number skills and adding by having each group of 4-6 students stand alternately for hot or cold lunch. They tell you the totals. Both added together should equal the number in the group.

USE OF HOOKS To take roll, have each student's name on a hook on a bulletin board. As they come in, they turn their name over. Names still showing will be marked absent. Later on, a student volunteer turns them all back around again.

CHALKBOARD

If you have students who leave first thing in the morning for a special area teacher, instruct them to always sign in and indicate their choices of lunch on the chalkboard before they leave.

MEET STUDENTS

Meet and greet each child at the door. As they pass by, they say either "hot" or "cold" to signify hot or cold lunch. Only mark the smaller number of the two groups. (By a matter of elimination, the rest, minus any absentees, will be the other group.) You will have your count done before the bell rings, saving lots of time and the need to call off each student by name.

SELF-MARKING SHEET

Laminate a copy of the hot/cold lunch count sheet. Place it on a clipboard by the door. Students mark their own preferences as they arrive in the morning. You just copy it onto the office copy. Simply wash off the marks with a damp towel and you're ready for tomorrow.

COMPUTER PRINT OUT

Have the students check off the type of lunches on a computer print out as they come in. Read back quickly to ensure accuracy. Perhaps just read all of one choice while by a matter of elimination the rest must be the remaining choice.

A CAN

Have the same number of tongue depressors as you have students. As they come in, they put one in either the hot lunch, cold lunch, or no milk can. Check absentees against any left in the original can. The rest is a matter of counting the tongue depressors and jotting the numbers down on the attendance sheet. If their names are on them, attendance can be individualized.

ROW COUNT

Have one student from each row responsible for giving you their row's count. The student quickly walks down his/her row and asks each student's choice that day. Once again, the total number should equal the number of students assigned.

ON TASK

Have students start their journal writings or proofreading exercises as soon as they arrive. The teacher can then take a personal check on each student while the rest are on task with a meaningful activity.

(Attendance)

INFORMATIONAL INTERACTION

Use the first 5-10 minutes each day as a visit, sharing, news time. It gives the teacher time to interact on an informal basis with each student, while taking attendance at the same time.

INDEPENDENT ACTIVITY

Assign an independent activity, such as a proofreading exercise, each morning. During this independent work time, you can more leisurely take attendance.

VISUAL FUN

A simple, effective, visual, fun way to take lunch count can be incorporated into a train, boat, car, etc. bulletin board. Let's suppose you choose train cars. Put a student's name on each one. As students arrive in the morning, they put a strip of red paper in their car if they want hot lunch. They put a strip of blue paper in their car if they are taking cold lunch. No strip means they are absent. Take the count quickly off of the train. All you have to do is "train" the students to do it....

"This time, like all times, is a very good one, if we know what to do with it."

Ralph Waldo Emerson
The American Scholar
1837

**TEAM
TEACHING**

Team the lunch count with your teaching partner. One teacher is responsible for the cold lunch and absentee count. The other teacher is responsible for the hot lunch count. Adding the two together should equal the total class count. It is a good system of checks and balances. Student helpers and taking count at the door can be used to speed up the process. **(See example "A", p. 48)**

**STAND AND
COUNT OFF**

Have all hot lunch students stand. Have them count off by successive numbers as they sit down one at a time. The last number called is recorded on the sheet for hot lunch.

**ABSENT
STUDENT(S)**

Ask the class if they have seen ___(absent student)___. If not, you know they are not just late into the classroom from the coat hall, lavatory, office, or nurse's room.

**WHO'S
ABSENT**

Just ask the class who's absent. They are very accurate, and many times will be able to tell you "exactly" why they are gone.

**SPONGE
ACTIVITY**

As a sponge activity, give each student a math fact (3 X 9 = _____) as you take roll. It is a good review and efficient use of the time. A variation would be one of this week's spelling words. Be creative with the curriculum.

"Experience is what you get when you don't get what you want."

--Dan Stanford

NOTES:

"*A stitch in time saves nine.*"

Anonymous

TIME SAVER   Put your attendance sheet on your metal file cabinet with a magnet so that it is easy to find. Clipping it to a clipboard will also save you panicked minutes looking for the misplaced sheet.

USE OF CHAIRS   All chairs are placed on top of each student's desk at the end of the day. In the morning, any chair still on top of the desk after the bell rings signifies an absentee.

"All time is lost which might be better employed."

Proverb

ATTENDANCE COUNT - COLD LUNCH

A B	L M
C	N O
D E	P Q
F G	R S
H I	T U
J K	V, W, X, Y, Z

Chapter V - Student Jobs

TEACHER PLEASE NOTE: Please be aware that many of the ideas shared by teachers can and do transcend across several grade levels. Be sure to read all grades' suggestions in order to profit from the many other excellent ideas.

INTRODUCTION

This chapter presents a compiled list of student jobs. It is by no means complete, but may spark an idea you haven't tried or thought of.

Delegating duties develops responsibility for students and saves you time in not having to do them yourself.

Students get a feeling of independence, control, and positive self-esteem through assuming responsibilities.

(Student Jobs)

The following are job ideas that have been used successfully at the K-6 levels. Choose the ones that apply to your style, class, and grade level:

- assignment teacher
- assignment tracker
- assistant teacher
- audio-visual helper/film set up
- board cleaner
- bulletin board helpers
- bulletin board makers
- bus line leader
- calendar person
- class leader
- class secretary/recorder (writes daily assignments on chalkboard from plan book
- computer helper
- DAP (Developmental Activity Program) math manipulatives bags checker
- date checker keeps date current for paper headings
- desk checker
- door holders
- drink monitor at the fountain
- fans turned on and off for ventilation
- file clerk
- flag leader for the pledge
- greeter for visitors to the classroom
- hall/locker monitor/coat rack checker
- helper(s) for-the-day (does **all** jobs)
- homework helper
- lavatory monitors for noise, behavior, & litter
- library helper
- line leader
- luncher reads hot lunch menu each morning
- lunchroom helper
- light switch monitor
- messenger to run (walk) errands
- music person - readies books, materials (Use for any subject area)
- paper collectors
- paper passers
- peer tutors
- pencil sharpener
- plant/fish keepers
- poet of the week (joke, riddle, etc. 1 per day/week)
- recess, phy.ed. equipment handler (carries equipment, hands it out, collects it.

- room cleaner
- room duster
- room inspector
- room straighteners (books, games, puzzles
- rotator - rotates all jobs at end of the week
- row captain
- security agent opens, closes, and locks all windows each day
- sink cleaner (paste)
- song leader
- spelling helper to pronounce make-up tests
- sub helper to specifically help substitute teachers
- sub monitor for jobs of absent students
- substitute teacher helpers
- super teacher-monitors when teacher is out of room
- sweeping and vacuuming monitors
- textbook collectors
- textbook passers
- telephone answerer
- time keeper
- vacationer - no job
- wastebasket person
- weather person
- window monitor for weather, fire drills, etc.

* Everyone does his/her part without assigning jobs.

* Head person and 2 helpers do **all** jobs.

BEAR JOBS   Cut out bears for each job. The bears' hats have the job printed on them. The bow ties are separate and have the students' names on them. The bow ties are slipped into a slot on the bears' chests.

HELPING HANDS   Make a set of **"Helping Hands."** Put each child's name on a hand. Whenever you need a job done, draw a hand off the top of the pile, assign the job, and put the hand back on the bottom. Colored paper that has been laminated makes them very durable.

ROTATING BOARD   Set up a board to rotate students for jobs. The students' names are on cards placed on hooks. Simply remove a card and the next name appears under the job title. When the last card is used, replace the entire stack of cards and continue.

WHEEL   Make a wheel and divide it into the number of duties you want. Students' names are placed around the outside of the wheel on a bulletin board. As the wheel is rotated, a different student's name appears next to each job. After all the students have had every job one time, the names are changed for the next group of students. Mark the starting position so you'll remember when it has gone full circle. It saves time changing names all the time. A turn of the wheel, and you're done.

JOB BULLETIN BOARD   Make a permanent bulletin board with jobs listed. Cut slots in tagboard to slip name tags in and out of next to the jobs. Mark the duty on the back of the name tags so students do not get the same job all the time and so everyone gets a chance to do each job at least once during the year. Make up a simple number key to speed this record keeping up.

CLOTHESPINS   Have a large class list on tagboard. Put the jobs required on clothespins. Clip the proper clothespin next to the name of your choice. It is easy to use, lasts all year, and the clothespins are reusable each year. **"It's a snap."** Title the chart: **"Snap To It."**

HELPER'S CHART   List all the jobs on a **"Helper's Chart."** St. Paul Book sells one that can be written on with grease pen marker and washed off each week. You could laminate your own, custom designed, helper chart.

(Student Jobs)

BULLETIN BOARD CALENDAR
Students make all markers for the bulletin board calendar. They put the numerals on 4-leaf clovers for March, for instance. It is their job to put the correct numeral up each day.

FUN RESPONSI-BILITY
Rotate the responsibility to bring in a poem, riddle, etc. to share each morning. It fosters memorization, responsibility, getting up in front of a group, and parent involvement.

MONITORS
Lunch monitors can excuse rows that are ready to wash hands and line up. They also can have the responsibility of monitoring behavior through the hallway. It makes them more aware of pre-requisites to lunch.

ONE HELPER PER DAY
Eliminate charts and time wasted in assigning student jobs all together. Just have one helper each day who does **all** the little extra duties. Take a more informal approach.

"Many hands make light work."

Proverbs

EMPLOYMENT SERVICE	List all room jobs on an **"Employment Service Poster."** This can be tied into a theme for career education.
FOOTPRINTS	Make a **"Hop to it and Help"** chart with students' names on footprints. They keep their footprint next to the job for a month to save time doing it each week.
DUTY BOARD	List all students' jobs on a **"Duty Board."** The names are hung on a hook below each designation. Change each duty every two weeks during the class meeting. Children can choose their class presidents, and the teacher chooses the duties based on good work habits the preceding two weeks.
A JOB PER STUDENT	Have a job for each student in the class. Rotate at the end of each week. Move the names, from the hook eyes, one position. The students' names are on round cardboard with a hole punched in the top. Some jobs are assigned to two students. The jobs get done quicker, are still done if there is an absence, and students learn to share and work together.
CHALKBOARD	Attach cut-outs with students' jobs on them to the chalkboard. Just write their names under them. It is very easy to erase and write the next choices on the board.
JOBS AS PRIVILEGES	The teacher assigns the jobs by the past two week's responsible performance. It is a privilege to have a duty. Those who did not have a job the last two-week period may stand up when they hear a job called off that they would like. They get first pick by the teacher.
BETTER PERFORMANCE	Keeping their assigned jobs longer allows them to really know and remember to do their jobs better. Don't switch them too often before they really get efficient.
RANDOM SELECTION	Place all students' names in a folder with the jobs labeled on the front. Randomly pull a name from the folder to assign that particular job. The materials last the entire year.
CLASS LIST	Assign jobs weekly by just going down the class list in order. It is fair, everyone gets a chance to do **both** the fun and unpopular duties, and it is fast.
JOB EVALUATION	Make up a quick number evaluation form. Individual students evaluate the work of others and themselves. **(See example "A", p. 61)**

(Student Jobs)

100% REWARD
Anytime students get 100%, or correct their own papers for 100%, they become helpers to teach the concepts to students having trouble. Peer tutoring is a positive job. have.

STUDENT SELECTS STUDENT
Let the student select the next person to fill his/her job. Someone must be chosen who has not done that particular job before. Decision making can be taught here.

CHOOSING JOBS
Let students choose the jobs they want. Have a sign up list under each job. Encourage them to take their fair turns at them all. Go down the list until everyone has had a chance, crossing them off as you go.

YOUR ROOM
Put up a sign reading: **"This is a self-cleaning classroom---you clean it yourself."**

DESK CHECKER
Assign a desk checker. He/she hands out **"Condemned"** warnings. A second warning results in dumping the desk out on the floor by the teacher.

END-OF-DAY
To clean the room, line up one half of the class on each end of the room facing each other. They walk slowly to the middle, straightening desks and picking up the floor. It is a good way to end the last 5 minutes of the day.

MONITORS
Assign lavatory monitors for noise, behavior, and litter.

ASSISTANT TEACHER
Have a student become your **"Assistant Teacher."** Place a "special" desk next to yours. Assign a top student to this responsibility. He/she may be given tasks such as correcting papers, recording, timing tests, helping other students with questions, tutoring small groups, monitoring classroom when teacher is out, etc..

INDEPENDENCE
Pretest at the beginning of the school year for top spellers. These can go **"Independent"** on their spelling and give each other the weekly tests as they are ready for them. Check at different periods of time to assure quality. Other students can prove themselves ready for this by getting six 100s in a row.

COMPUTER HELPERS
Select a couple good computer students to help other students when the whole class goes to the computer lab. They help with problems and assist without doing the work for their classmates. They feel good about having a more responsible position, and you have an easier time getting around to everyone.

THEME	Set your duty board to a theme. Think of catchy titles for the jobs. For example, a ship theme for the **"crew"** could include 1st lieutenant, deck swabbers, communications expert, supply sergeant, etc. A movie theme might have sound specialists, public relations, assistant director, lighting technician, etc..
STUDENT	Assign a bulletin board for 2 to 4 students every 3 to 4 weeks. They plan, organize, put it up, and take it down. It can be related to an academic project or their choice. Have the design approved before construction begins. Ownership of the room, art skills, teamwork, and knowledge review are just a few of the spinoffs.
CARD SHUFFLE	Have student names on 3 x 5 cards. Shuffle the cards and randomly assign them to jobs and put their cards in library pockets with the job description on the outside. Change them every week. Those names not used get drawn first next week. When all names are used, reshuffle the pack and start over.
STUDENT IN CHARGE	Have three major jobs: Chalkboard, chairs, and floor. Everyone helps, but one student is in charge of the quality of the work done by others.
LIST TO BE DONE	List the work that needs to be done on the chalkboard and have the students just sign up for the ones that they want. Have one period a week scheduled in just to clean desks and the room.
ROTATOR	Assign a rotator to rotate all the jobs at the end of the week. They do the physical work as well as the procedure planning.
SECOND IN COMMAND	Assign a second in command to take over the jobs of any absentee. This eliminates choosing in the middle of the day. It's already in place.
FILE CLERK	Assign a file clerk to keep track of student folders, collecting and returning them as required. Papers all put face up saves you sorting time.
ASSIGNMENT TRACKER	Assign an assignment tracker who writes all assignments on the chalkboard. He/she may be made responsible for tracking delinquent and absentee assignments, also.

(Students Jobs)

ON VACATION Assign a job called, **"On Vacation."** This person doesn't have any job that period. It provides a nice break for a job well-done.

LUNCHROOM Assign lunchroom table washers for the cafeteria. Custodians and cooks will welcome good help.

SUB HELPER Ask a **"sub helper"** to help answer questions for the substitute teacher. This responsible position is kept until after a sub is used, then rotated.

RECORDER A recorder writes daily assignments onto the chalkboard from your plan book. The more involvement, the better!

HOMEWORK HELPER A homework helper fills in forms for all absent students and puts his/her name and telephone number on the assignment sheet. Absent students can call the **Homework Helper** for any assignment questions or clarifications. If absentees are sick over two days, get-well cards are in order. Get make-up work to their homes so it doesn't get stacked up.

LIBRARY PERSON A library person selects 30 books each month for the class to use for free or open reading time. They make better choices than the teacher. Set them up on a table display. Discuss them to promote involvement.

PEER TUTOR Students are responsible for teaching any absent students what was missed. It is good management for you and educationally sound for both the peer tutors and the absent students.

RETEACHING Use top students to help reteach and reinforce others in areas of weakness. Peer teaching can be rewarded by cutting down on the tutors' work load to make up for the time they spend with their peers.

CLASS PARTY

Planning a class party? Assign three students who are able to do the total planning. They can organize and get other students involved in sub groups. Give them a limited 15 minutes out of class time to get organized, and the rest they do on their own.

STUDENT GOVERNMENT

Students are assigned the responsibility for School/Student Government. They give weekly reports on student council and updates on school news each day from their sources and the office bulletin.

INDEPENDENT TEACHING

Strive for lots of independent teaching. Students can learn what has to be done and take the responsibility and ownership to get it finished on time. They should be able to make decisions about pacing. Many students thrive and perform at their best under these conditions.

"Easy is the task when many hands share the toil."

Bruce Bigelow

NOTES:

"Never before have we had so little time in which to do so much."

F. D. Roosevelt

EVERYONE CHIPS IN	Don't waste time with charts and assigning jobs. Everyone is expected to chip in and help. You can ask students who have finished their work early to do some work that is needed.
STUDENT OF THE WEEK	Establish a **"Student of the Week."** This person gets to do all of the jobs such as messenger, line leader, shades, lights, paper collection, passbacks, etc..
GROUPS	Assign students to a group for a month. Desks are put together. Assign one student as the **"group monitor."** They do all the handing out and collecting of papers, and any other extra jobs such as making sure their group area is clean, chairs are in order, assignments are finished, etc.
INCREASE SELF-ESTEEM	Choose the lower-ability child for different jobs. This will increase self-esteem, confidence, trustworthiness, responsibility. and dependability.
ROTATE DUTIES	Rotate duties so that everyone does every job sometime throughout the school year.
TWO NAMES	List two names on each school day of the room calendar. These are the helpers for the day. Students can exchange if they are absent or have prior commitments and cannot stay in at noon or after school to help.
TWO STARS	Put two stars next to any job which requires two workers. It helps when handing out the jobs to remember.
CHOOSE A JOB	The "student of the week" gets to choose one "work job" off the duty board and the Phy. Ed. choice day activity for the week.
HELPER-OF THE-DAY	Establish a **"Helper-of-the-Day."** Any question a student has, they ask the helper-of-the-day first. This relieves you of some of the constant "needs." The helper is not to give answers to problems but helps explain how to do the problem and answers other types of questions.
PEER TUTORS LOWER GRADES	Sixth graders can be excellent peer tutors for lower grades. They can read to them, write their dictated stories, etc.. All parties gain through these interactions.

HALL MONITOR

A hall monitor checks on coats, wraps, and boots. Have them check after everyone is sitting down after the bell rings. A cleaning cart to roam the halls with during noon hour elicits lots of positive compliments and good feelings.

WASTE BASKET HELPER

Establish a waste basket helper for wrappers of outdoor treats. If you have snack break outside, wrappers will be easily collected. Inside, the basket can be passed too!

INSPECTOR

The inspector at the end of the day, checks each row for a clean area and dismisses them. The inspector is then responsible for anything on the floor after everyone has left.

WINDOW/DOOR PERSON

Assign a window and door person to be responsible for opening and shutting them, dependent upon the weather, fire drill, or normal operation.

LIBRARY HELPER

Use a library helper to return the classes' library books all at once. Set up a collection point on a cart or in a tub. This eliminates all that unsupervised traffic.

EQUIPMENT HANDER

The equipment handler for recess equipment hands out equipment in an orderly fashion so it isn't a "grab for all." He/she gives pieces to the quietest person with their hand raised.

WEATHER REPORTER

The day's weather conditions and ramifications are reported by the weather reporter. He/she charts the temperature on a graph. Talk about science concepts.

DOOR HOLDER

Assign door holders. They come to the front of the line and hold the door from slamming into the line, and then they fall into the back of the line until the next door.

FIVE PIECES

Say, **"Everyone pick up 5 pieces of scraps off the floor."** Encourage **"we versus me."** We help each other even if we didn't make the mess.

AFTER SCHOOL HELPERS

If you have students who do not get on their bus until 10-15 minutes after school is out, use this potential by having them help you in the room for a few minutes after school. They can clean, prepare materials for the next day, etc. It sure beats unproductive behavior, just hanging out for the busses to come.

NAME_____

ROOM CLEAN UP EVALUATION

1   2   3   4   5

Assigned Area

_____

My Area

_____

Total

NOTES:

"*Time and the tide wait for no man.*"

Proverbs

Chapter VI - Behavior

TEACHER PLEASE NOTE: Please be aware that many of the ideas shared by teachers can and do transcend across several grade levels. Be sure to read all grades' suggestions in order to profit from the many other excellent ideas.

INTRODUCTION

Behavior is a learned experience which will either be productive or non-productive. The school has a great influence on the child in helping to develop productive behavior:

You have a choice to do one of the following:
1. Punish and/or control a behavior.
2. To help change the behavior of a student to be productive.

By using behavior modification or through counseling experience, students can learn to be self-directed.

Basic principles that need to be addressed are as follows:
1. Help develop high self-esteem; **"I can do!"** Remember, **"Success builds success."**
2. Separate any undesirable behavior of a student from the "student:" attack the undesirable behavior, not the child.
3. "Discipline with dignity." Respect the feelings of a student.
4. Be "Pro active" not "reactive."
5. Use the least severe method to deal effectively at the appropriate level of misbehavior.
6. To be effective, **time** and effort will need to be given to more difficult behaviors if change is to be expected.

This chapter offers a variety of suggestions to deal with and to help change inappropriate behaviors.

NOTES:

"*Problems are only opportunities with thorns on them.*"

--*Hugh Miller*
  Snow on the Wind (St. Martin's)

UN-LINE-UP

Have an **"Un-line-up."** Whoever can follow the five guidelines for the hallway can pass on their own. Others line up with the teacher. The five rules are:
1) walk
2) stay on the right side of the hall
3) keep hands to self
4) take one step at a time
5) quiet

PARENTS INFORMED

Explain your discipline procedure to all the parents during the first Open House. Have the child, then, phone the parent in your presence with the explanation and solution for the problem. You do not need to talk to the parent unless you disagree with something that is said.

CHALKBOARD

Number one through ten on the chalkboard (1-2-3-4-5-6-7-8-9-10). If the class is out of control, erase the 10, and so on. If the class is really good, add a number; 10, 11, 12... At the end of the day, add the number to the running class total. When they get 50 or 100 points, provide a class reward.

OUT OF THE ROOM

When out of the room, have the total class act as **"Checkers."** All watch each other. One warning is permissible. The second time deserves a report to the teacher. Perhaps work in a "+" reward if **all** the class agrees.

NONVERBAL SIGNAL

A nonverbal signal of inappropriateness can be accomplished by writing **"10"** on the board. This stands for the number of minutes of recess for the day. The number can be erased and changed up or down depending upon the classes' response.

TIME "+" or "-"

Time students save or waste is added to or subtracted from break time.

PUPPET SIGNAL

Use a puppet to redirect students back to you. Carry on a conversation with the puppet. The puppet can give directions and comments. This visual will help get their attention before you begin to talk.

TIMEOUT

Use an egg timer for a **"timeout"** consequence. The student has to sit out for three minutes and comes back on his/her own.

(Behavior)

THINK ABOUT... A fast, easy, no discussion discipline is to simply tell the students to put their heads down on their arms at their desk and **"Think about what they should be doing and how they could do it better the next time."** Make it a mandatory 5 minutes per infraction.

PROXIMITY SUPPORT Stand close to a student who needs extra support. Assign him/her to a desk near you until he/she is more comfortable with the classroom.

QUIET GAME Play a **"quiet game."** If a student talks out of turn, put a smilie face on the board which means the teacher wins a point.

BEHAVIOR PLAN A consistent behavior plan for several groups of children who see many different teachers can be established with **behavior folders**. These are initialed and negative behavior is keyed with a number to explain the problem. The reports are sent home each week for parent signatures. "No initials" may be rewarded with a stamp or sticker. **(See example "A", p. 77)**

END-OF-THE-DAY At the end of the day, read part of a story to calm students down before they go home. It helps the scurry atmosphere of running to the bus line and even carries through on the bus or the walk home. Singing of songs is another nice calm way to end the session.

"Education does not mean teaching people to know what they do not know; it means teaching them to behave as they do not behave."

John Ruskin
1819-1900

ENVIRONMENT THEME

Set your room up as a theme. Establish the room as a ship. Call it the U.S.S. Friendship. You are the captain. They are the crew. Living this fantasy increases motivation and establishes esprit de corps. Portholes on a bulletin board can highlight star papers. You can hold a Ship's Meeting once a week to choose the duty board and discuss new business using Robert's Rules of Order. A three-step discipline plan can take the form of a "working bulletin board." Label it DON'T WALK THE PLANK. Student names are on swords. If their sword is on the plank for an infraction, they line up last. If they fall off the end into the sharks, they have to write a paragraph with an explanation and a plan of change. The third step is, their name is placed on "Teacher's Black List" and they lose all privileges. Each time they end up in the sharks in the same 6-week period, adds another paragraph to their shark contract assignment. Discipline, being a two-edged sword, requires a positive, also. Establish a throttle for 1/4, 1/2, and Full Speed. Make a Sink the Pirate Ship that disappears by 8 increments. They sink the ship one or more notches at a time by "Taking Their Best Shot." Each sink earns a 1/2 hour surprise period. These can be saved up for larger blocks of time, too. Decorate with sea decor. Art lessons might include designing a flag and pictures of sea creatures. Small groups of desks can be lifeboats with a captain for each.

Living the journey of education makes it more real, meaningful, and fun.

MOVEMENT OF STUDENTS

Try to control the number of students moving at any one time. Move them by a row or a group at a time versus the total class all at once. This cuts down on noise and traffic congestion.

JOINT PLAN

If two or more classes have a common problem with equipment, or playground space, for example, choose one student from each class to meet and come up with a fair plan.

CHOICE

Set up a structured behavior program for your class. Have steps of consequences, parent notification, and student inservice. Emphasize that student behavior is a **"Choice"-- theirs. (See examples "B" and "C", pp. 78-79)**

(BEHAVIOR)

TIME TO THINK	Establish a **Time to Think** room **(TTT Room)**. It is a half hour after school detention program. It is a school project where parents are informed, teachers rotate the assignment between them, and students write up contracts of behavior change. The bussing situation doesn't become an excuse for not staying after school, because it is agreed upon school policy. **(See example "D", p. 80)**
BEHAVIOR SHEET	Set up a **"behavior sheet"** which is sent back and forth each night for the parent to sign. Assignments late can also be handled the same way.
SHOW/INDICATE LOVE	Children need love to be loved. Have them do many extra things to feel important, busy, and feel needed. Give students a choice of a **hug** or a **handshake** as a positive reward. **Take the child by the hand and walk with him/her** if he/she can't manage to behave himself/herself. Dress as a role-model, not as a student yourself.
TELLING VERSUS TATTLING	Explain the difference between telling (tattling) and reporting a situation that might hurt someone's feelings or cause physical harm. If they are telling, ask them to write a note about the incident. If it is important, they will; if not, they won't bother.
5-MINUTE TIME OUT	Tired of tattling? If it's important enough to complain about, it's important enough for **both** of the parties to take an automatic 5-minute time out and talk with each other face-to-face without the teacher being involved. They solve the problem themselves 90% of the time. The teacher decides when the time out should be held and does not get involved unless the problem cannot be settled by themselves. If the teacher gets involved, there is an automatic penalty for one or both. This increases responsibility and decreases dependability on the teacher.

"Expect people to be better than they are; it helps them to become better. But don't be disappointed when they are not; it helps them to keep trying."

-- Merry Browne in National Inquirer

CLASS GOALS Establish class goals at the start of the school year. Keep coming back to these goals during the year and have students share about the things that are keeping us from our goals. Talk to the students as individuals and emphasize that they are individuals who are "becoming." They should perceive themselves as being able to think and be responsible.

TIME-OUT Use short **"time-out"** periods and then develop decision-making skills for what, why, and how to prevent the behavior the next time. **(See example "E", p. 81)**

THINK TIME To relieve anxiety, set up a non-defensive think time by asking the errant student to step out into the hallway and to come back in as soon as they are ready. Keep him/her out a very short time. You may even step out with him/her and talk about the infraction. Explain the procedure at the beginning of the year so that students are not caught off guard.

DESK ARRANGEMENT Have all the desks face the walls in one large square. It cuts down on distractions. Instruction is given by bringing their chairs to the center of the room in a group.

SELF-EVALUATION Students can benefit by **self-evaluation** check lists. Their levels of consciousness were higher through participation. **(See examples "F", "G", "H", and "I", pp. 82-85)**

NATURAL CONSEQUENCES Use as many "logical and natural consequences" as possible. If there is a mess, clean it up. If they are late, **they** write a note and date it. This record is for them to keep and is used at conferences to come up with a plan for improvement.

POST OUT-OF-THE-ROOM RULE Place a sign next to the room clock for maximum visibility. On it have the room rule: **"When the teacher is not present, all students are to remain seated."**

"It's better to build children than repair men."

NOTES:

"*Time: that which man is always trying to kill, but which ends in killing him.*"

Herbert Spencer
1820-1903

QUICK ACTION   Try to identify and change behaviors quickly **before** they become bigger problems. Try to address them with parents **before** conference time if they are serious. Swift and sure handling of problems will set a precedence and not allow them to get out-of-hand.

CONSISTENCY   You must be 100% consistent and follow up if you say you're going to do something. Use cues to help redirect students' behavior.

FLEXIBILITY   Don't treat every group the same. The type of group you have determines what and how you do things.

MODEL POSITIVE COMMENTS   Use more positive, verbal encouragements. The power of correct models encourages others to do the same.

SIGNAL INTERFERENCE   If a student is doing something wrong, look to a student near him/her and state aloud the proper behavior displayed. It gives positive reinforcement to the obeying child and points out the problem to the wrong-doer without embarrassing him/her.

ENCOURAGE-MENT   "Encouragement" is far more powerful in dealing with individuals and groups than "praise."
(See examples "J" and "K", pp. 86-87)

GLASSER and CANTER   Use Glasser's Reality Therapy-A New Approach to Psychiatry, New York, New York, Harper and Row, 1975. This is also part of Canter's Assertive Discipline, Canters and Associates, Inc., Dept. CB, P.O. Box 2113, Santa Monica, CA 90406. Telephone (213) 395-3221. Ask for item #1016 @ $6.95.

CHOICES   An effective philosophy is to give the student a choice and a consequence. You will need to talk about the two items:
   1) Who's losing by the choice?
   2) Who's responsible for **your** behavior? (They are!)
Then have some examples to share and discuss like, **"You can do the work or sit out and do the work at break time or during the noon hour." (See example "L", p. 88)**

RESPECT

Behavior revolves around the teacher's personality. Behavior is how you relate to the students. Give a lot of respect to them. Students want to do well. You help build this work habit and they start to grow and improve as you encourage them and reinforce them. Everything starts to snowball in a positive atmosphere. Individual conferences, a good sense of humor, and encouraging students to talk to you makes it like one big family. Students can and do learn to control themselves.

RESPECT THE STUDENT

Don't call out the name of the student, as it is like a public embarrassment. Also, do not praise a single student by name for the same reason. Treat them like adults.

DATA RECORD

Keep dated discipline records on students for larger infractions. It is useful for hard data when talking to parents or for referrals to get special help.

GRID CHART

Keep a simple grid chart for behavior problems. No comments needed. Just a letter behind the student's name: **L = late, T = talking, F = fighting, etc.** Set it up the first day of class. It is excellent data for parent-teacher-child conferences.

CARD SYSTEM

Use a card system for infractions. Alphabetized recipe cards work well to date and make notes on. These are then discussed at the parent-teacher-child conferences.

STUDENT'S PLAN

Making students responsible for their own behavior can be furthered with individual behavior plans made out by the students. These can then be used as a matter of record and discussed at parent-teacher-child conferences.

I.C.M.M. CLUB

Establish an **I.C.M.M. Club - (I Can Manage Myself).** Laminate 3 x 5 cards with the insignia and tape to those desks who have earned them every two weeks. They can be taken away and earned again. Certain privileges are bestowed such as lining up first, use of certain learning materials (games), etc.

STUDENTS RATE CLASS

Students rate the class 1 to 10 on their own behavior. This self-evaluation is a positive step in decision making.

FIVE RULES

School rules can fit into five main areas. There is no reason to play games or set up specific rules for every specific behavior. Boil everything down into:

1. Respect
2. Responsibility
3. Distractions
4. Destruction
5. Safety

4-STEP SYSTEM

Have a **4-step** discipline plan. Know what each step is and be consistent. An example might be:

1. Give a look
2. Give a look and point at them
3. Walk over to the student
4. Walk over and put your hand on his/her shoulder

COLOR CARD SYSTEM

If you use the card system where students flip a series of colored cards in library pockets, successive measures might be:

first card	=	starting position
second card	=	warning
third card	=	10 minutes in at noon
fourth card	=	30 minutes in at noon
fifth card	=	30 minutes in at noon and a letter to parents by the child

Record the episode and date it on the back of the 3rd, 4th, and 5th cards.

STUDENTS' OWN RECORD

For students having a problem getting work completed, give them a week's schedule sheet which they fill in day-by-day. Pupils "X" out the subject when completed, and the sheets go home on Friday to be signed and returned on Monday. It provides focus, visual reinforcement, a data record, and public relations with parents. **(See example "M", p. 89)**

COOPERATIVE GROUPS

Use cooperative learning groups. Turn the problem over to the "team." If the team control doesn't work, talk to the student privately. The next step would be a call home if needed.

CIRCLE GROUP Conduct a circle group discussion as needed to form new rules, and especially to discuss the "why" you need them.

ONE-TO-ONE Do a lot of one-to-one conferencing with students. Knowing students on a one-to-one basis solves a lot of discipline problems before they start. Schedule in time for this daily.

T.E.S.A. **T.E.S.A.** really helps awareness through training and application. **(Teacher Expectation and Student Achievement)** Training for local trainers along with further information may be received from:

     Phi Delta Kappa
     P.O. Box 789
     8th and Union St.
     Bloomington, Indiana 47402

ESTABLISHING RULES Make rule-setting at the beginning of the year a learning experience. Have students decide the rules they want in the room. Make a master list. After trying to live within these several rules, periodically talk about them and weed out the bad ones. After a few weeks, it should boil down to a few (no more than 3 to 5) general rules that cover most everything. Ideas might include:

     * Do Your Best
     * Use Good Manners
     * Get Assignments In On Time
     * Act As A Family
     * Show Respect
     * NO Name Calling
     * Don't Talk When Someone Is In Front
     * Stay Seated If Teacher Is Out Of Room

3 R's Teach the 3 R's: **Respect, Relax, and Rapport.** Respect for self and others is taught and lived by for the entire year. Establish the theme through discussions during the first week of school.

GUIDELINES In place of class rules, use a set of guidelines to be followed. Discuss and establish during the first few weeks of school. After that, deal directly one-on-one with problems.

ONE RULE Keep it simple, just have ONE RULE: **"You can do anything in the classroom as long as it doesn't interfere with anyone's learning."**

EXPECTATIONS Students usually live up to your expectations. Set your expectations high and let them know what they are. Expectations need to be reasonable.

CHILD'S LEVEL Stoop or sit down so that you talk to children at eye level, not above them.

PICTURES FOR REMINDERS Have stacks of pictures with simple messages on them. Run off copies. **(See example "N" and "O", pp. 90-91)**

PROXIMITY CONTROL Sit in the back of the bus on field trips. This breaks up the usual problems, lets you command a view of the entire bus without them knowing if you are watching or not, and students must remain seated when the bus stops so that you can walk up the aisle to lead or give directions.

FOUR GOALS OF MISBEHAVIOR You gain a lot of time by having good to excellent behavior of your students. After behavior is in place (self-discipline) learning really improves and time can be saved from then on.

Most students will respond to emphasis on their good behavior through positive statements. However, you must deal with the 3 to 5% of any school population who fall into the **"Four Goals of Misbehavior:"**
1. Attention
2. Power
3. Revenge
4. Helplessness

These students cause teachers to spend 90% of their time on disciplining them. To understand these students better, read:

1. Dinkmeyer, D. & Gary McKoy, Systematic Training for Effective Teachers, American Guidance SErvice, Circle Pines, MN 55014.

2. Dreikus, Rudolf, M.D. & Bernice Bronia Grunwald, Maintaining Sanity in the Classroom-Classroom Management Technique.

NOTES:

"Being a spectator not only deprives one of participation, but also leaves one's mind free for unrelated activity. If academic learning does not engage students, something else will."

--John Goodlad (1983)

Dear Parents/Guardians,

The first/second grade team has set certain goals which we will strive to help your children reach this year. Some students are very close to mastery in these goals. Others will need help and encouragement in reaching them. The chart below will allow you as parents/guardians to see how your child is progressing.

If a child exhibits the desired behavior, his chart will not be initialed. If he does not, a teacher will, after necessary warnings, initial his chart on the day of the undesirable behavior. She will note, by number, which goal he/she has not reached that day.

Any child who has only 1 or 2 initials per week will be rewarded with a stamp. If a child has no signatures for the week, he/she will receive a sticker. The chart will come home in his <u>Thursday folder</u> every Thursday afternoon and is to be <u>returned signed on Friday morning.</u> Because of our Thursday take home schedule, the chart will run from Friday morning to Thursday afternoon. PLEASE be sure to look at it and sign in the provided space.

We thank you in advance for your support in this endeavor to help your child to be the best student that he/she can be!

GOALS:

1. Works quietly and independently.
2. Completes all work to the best of his/her ability and turns it in on time.
3. Listens and follows directions.
4. Brings necessary materials and is prepared for each class.
5. Exhibits self-control.
6. Controls talking.

*** Your signature indicates you have seen the behavior sheet.

MONTH	Friday	Monday	Tuesday	Wednesday	Thursday	REWARD	Parent Signature
Week 2-2 to 2-8	2	5	6	7	8		
Week 2-9 to 2-15	9	12	13	14	15		
Week 2-16 to 2-22	16	19 President's Day	20	21	22		
Week 2-23 to 3-1	23	26	27	28	1		
Week 3-2 to 3-8	2	5	6	7	8		
Week 3-9 to 3-15	9	12	13	14	15		

GAGE ELEMENTARY
SCHOOL

1300 N.W. 40th St., Rochester, MN 55901 • 507-281-607?

Dear Parents/Guardians:

In order to guarantee your child, and all the students in our classrooms, the excellent learning climate they deserve, we are utilizing the following Discipline Plan.

Philosophy:

We believe all our students can behave appropriately in our classrooms. We will tolerate no student stopping us from teaching and/or student from learning.

Our Class Rules:

1. Be prepared for class (assignments done, materials needed).
2. Be seated, listen to lessons, and follow directions.
3. Have appropriate behavior.
4. Keep hands, feet, objects to yourself.
5. Abide by Gage rules for break, lunchroom, playground and halls.

If a Student Chooses To Break A Rule:

1st consequence - warning - name on clipboard

2nd consequence - one check after name - 15 minutes make up time

3rd consequence - two checks after name - 30 minutes make up time and phone conference with parents

4th consequence - three checks - 30 minutes plus conference with parents and principal

Severe disruption- immediately to principal - conference at school with parents

Students Who Behave Will Earn:

A class popcorn party, gum day in the classroom, extra break time, positive note to parents, special activity afternoon.

It is your child's best interest that we work together in his/her schooling. We will thus be in close contact with you regarding your child's progress in our classrooms. Please sign the tear-off and have your child bring it with him/her to school. If you have any questions or comments, please feel free to call us or write them on the tear-o

Sincerely,

I have read and understood the Discipline Plan for your classroom.

Student Signature   Parent/Guardian Signature

DETENTION SLIP

_____

is to remain after school on

_____

for _____ minutes for the

following:

_____Incomplete Work

_____Directions not followed

_____Inappropriate behavior

_____Physically bothering others

_____School rules not minded

_____ Teacher

_____

Parent Signature

DETENTION SLIP

_____

is to remain after school on

_____

for _____ minutes for the

following:

_____Incomplete Work

_____Directions not followed

_____Inappropriate behavior

_____Physically bothering others

_____School rules not minded

_____ Teacher

_____

Parent Signature

DETENTION SLIP

_____

is to remain after school on

_____

for _____ minutes for the

following:

_____Incomplete Work

_____Directions not followed

_____Inappropriate behavior

_____Physically bothering otehrs

_____School rules not minded

_____ Teacher

_____

Parent Signature

DETENTION SLIP

_____

is to remain after school on

_____

for _____ minutes for the

following:

_____ Incomplete Work

_____Directions not followed

_____Inappropriate behavior

_____Physically bothering others

_____School rules not minded

_____ Teacher

_____

Parent Signature

NAME_____ Date_____

Please answer the following questions as honestly and carefully as possible. Use complete sentences.

1. Where and when did the problem happen? _____

_____

2. Who was involved? _____

_____

3. Explain what happened during the incident. _____

_____

_____

4. Did your behavior break our class rules? Which one(s)? _____

_____

_____

5. Did your behavior help you or anyone else? _____

_____

_____

6. What steps do you think should be taken as a result of this problem? _____

_____

_____

7. How do you plan to change the problem and your behavior? _____

_____

_____

_____   _____
Student's Name/Date   Teacher Name/Date

SIXTH GRADE ACTION PLAN

Rule Not Followed: _____

Consequence: _____

Time: _____

Date: _____

My Plan of Action: _____

_____

_____

_____

_____

_____

_____

_____

<u>MUST BE AT LEAST 50 WORDS AND WRITTEN IN COMPLETE SENTENCES.</u>

_____
Student Signature

_____
Teacher Signature

	Mon.	Tue.	Wed.	Thur.	Fri.
1. I whisper when I have something to say.					
2. I use my personal working space and keep it clean.					
3. I raise my hand to talk.					
4. I don't make funny sounds.					
5. I listen and follow directions.					

TOTAL POINTS:

82

MONDAY

TUESDAY

WEDNESDAY

THURSDAY

FRIDAY

NAME:

1. Name on paper

2. Whisper during work time

3. Tie shoelaces

4. Clean personal space

5. Push chair into desk

6. Follow directions

7. Save funny sounds for recess

8. Follow bathroom, lunch, drink rules

TOTAL GOALS:

RUN THAT BALL!!!!!

	Mon.		Tue.		Wed.		Thur.		Fri.		TOTAL
1. I raise my hand to talk	1	2	1	2	1	2	1	2	1	2	
2. I whisper if I must share (work periods)	1	2	1	2	1	2	1	2	1	2	
3. I keep my personal space clean	1	2	1	2	1	2	1	2	1	2	
4. I follow directions Name on all papers, etc.	1	2	1	2	1	2	1	2	1	2	
5. I tie my shoelaces	1	2	1	2	1	2	1	2	1	2	
6. I save funny sounds for recess	1	2	1	2	1	2	1	2	1	2	
7. I use good manners Thank you & Please	1	2	1	2	1	2	1	2	1	2	

DATE _____

NAME _____

84

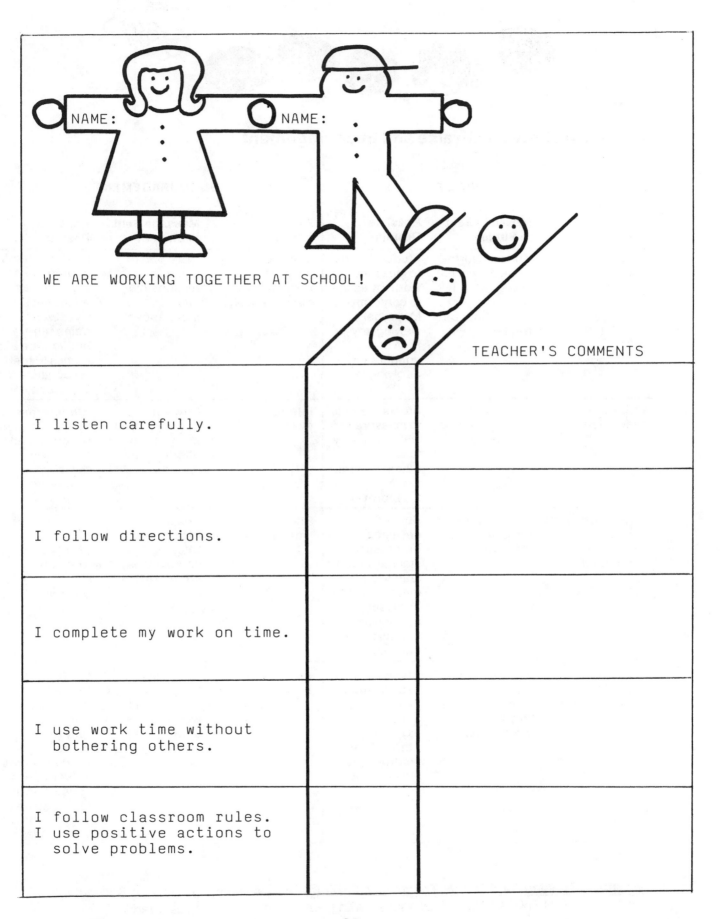

NAME:

NAME:

WE ARE WORKING TOGETHER AT SCHOOL!

TEACHER'S COMMENTS

I listen carefully.		
I follow directions.		
I complete my work on time.		
I use work time without bothering others.		
I follow classroom rules. I use positive actions to solve problems.		

Chart 3

Differences between Praise and Encouragement

	PRAISE			ENCOURAGEMENT	
Focus	**Message Sent to Student**	**Possible Results**	**Focus**	**Message Sent to Student**	**Possible Results**
1. External control.	You are worthwhile only when you do what I want. You cannot be trusted.	Student learns to measure worth by ability to conform. May rebel, viewing any form of cooperation as giving in.	Student's ability to manage life constructively.	I trust you to become responsible and independent.	Student learns courage to be imperfect and willingness to try. Student gains self-confidence and comes to feel responsible for own behavior.
2. External evaluation.	To be worthwhile, you must please me.	Student learns to measure worth by ability to please others. Learns to fear disapproval.	Internal evaluation.	How you feel about yourself and your own efforts is most important.	Student learns to evaluate own progress and to make own decisions.
3. Reward is only for well-done, completed tasks.	To be worthwhile, you must meet my standards.	Student develops unrealistic standards and learns to measure worth by closeness to perfection. Learns to fear failure.	Effort and improvement.	You don't have to be perfect. Effort and improvement are important.	Student learns to accept efforts of self and others. Student develops desire to stay with tasks (persistence).
4. Self-elevation and personal gain.	You're the best. You must remain superior to others to be worthwhile.	Student learns to be overcompetitive, to get ahead at the expense of others. Feels worthwhile only when on top.	Assets, contributions, and appreciation.	Your contribution counts. We function better with you. We appreciate what you have done.	Student learns to use talents and efforts for good of all, not only for personal gain. Student learns to feel glad for successes of others as well as for own successes.

Chapter 3

Points to Remember

1. Encouragement is helping students believe in themselves and in their abilities.

2. Encouragement is a basic attitude toward yourself and other people.

3. Encouragement is different from praise. Praise goes to those who excel or come in first; encouragement can be given for any positive movement. Encouragement does not have to be earned.

4. Praise places a value judgment on the student. Encouragement focuses on the work or effort, treating the student with acceptance and respect.

5. Encouragement accepts students as they are, not as they could be.

6. Encouragement helps the learner develop the courage to be imperfect.

7. Mistakes are not failures. They can promote learning.

8. The first step in encouragement is to stop making negative comments about students.

9. Identify talents, assets, positive attitudes and goals. Every student has strengths.

10. Factors which discourage include:
- Negative expectations.
- Unreasonably high standards.
- Competition.
- Overambition.
- Double standards.

11. Be an asset finder, not a fault finder.

"TIME TO DECIDE"

NAME_____

**I can control my own actions when I need to.

1._____

2._____

3._____

4._____

5._____

6._____

7._____

8._____

9._____

10._____

11._____

12._____

13._____

DATE_____ NAME_____

MONDAY	TUESDAY	WEDNESDAY	THURSDAY	FRIDAY
Math	Math	Math	Math	Math
Spelling	Spelling	Spelling	Spelling	Spelling
Reading	Reading	Reading	Reading	Reading
Language	Language	Language	Language	Language
Extra	Extra	Extra	Extra	Extra

Student
_____

You were a super star today!

_____
Teacher

I understand why

You feel tired!

You were a good worker.

_____
Teacher

Student
_____

What a great week you had!

_____

Student
_____

You slipped this week.

_____
Teacher

IT'S BEEN A "HOPPY" DAY!!

YOU WERE HELPFUL!!

_____

Homework Award

presented to

Homework Award

presented to

_____   _____

Good for YOU!!!!!   Good for YOU!!!!!

Signed_____   Signed_____

Date_____   Date_____

91

Chapter VII - Organizing Students

TEACHER PLEASE NOTE: Please be aware that many of the ideas shared by teachers can and do transcend across several grade levels. Be sure to read all grades' suggestions in order to profit from the many other excellent ideas.

INTRODUCTION

Try to work yourself out of a job by building independent learners. Use multiple methods to organize the total group, small groups, partners, and individuals.

Establishing intrinsic values and using skills of independence will bring about more self-directed learning and higher academic skills.

Cooperative learning groups go a long way in establishing a collaborative classroom organization.

Whatever ideas you find in this chapter will help you organize students better.

NOTES:

*"Think ahead--plan ahead--be one step ahead
to prevent or save problems,"*

--Karen Heimer

MAJOR AREAS

Establish a team of four teachers in kindergarten. Each room is set up for one major area of instruction. Students rotate through the four areas with their same teacher. This allows you to equip each room with specific materials. The changing of rooms allows for a change of pace and recharges students. Four possible areas are Math, Perceptual Motor Skills and Music, Small Group Skills, and Self-Directed Learning Activities. Teachers plan together weekly.

TEAM TEACHING READING

Team teaching of reading can include special area teachers, educational aides, volunteers, etc. Eighty students can be broken down into six sub groups, with two reading groups per teacher. For planning, the groups are color-coded for an easy-to-read schedule.

ASSIGNED WORK AREAS

Assign areas to go to when assigned work is finished. Each child is given a shape (square, circle, rectangle, triangle, etc.) Then each area is posted with a like-symbol. Rotate the posted signs every few days.

STUDENT'S OWN WORK TIME

Teach and develop individual work time. Build in time for students to work on their own work. This will save you uncountable hours of direct instruction over the year, while students learn by doing.

STATIONS

Schedule station work for part of the day. Students move at their own pace/ability. Less time is wasted as more students are on task. You will have more time to help students on an individual basis by need. Four to five stations are a nice number to work with.

TEACH ORGANIZATION

Don't take it for granted that all children know how to clean desks and organize them. Actually, teach this as a lesson. Take it step-by-step.

DESK CHECK

Have students clean their desks regularly. Time is saved in their getting out their materials faster. Perhaps the **"desk fairy"** might visit every weekend to reward organization. (Don't forget that **YOU** are their best model!)

94

ORGANIZE DESK

To help students organize their desks, ask parents to send either checkbook boxes or a Velveeta Cheese Box. All the crayons and pencils are stored in these boxes. Larger boxes are not recommended, as they get filled up with many other unnecessary items.

STUDENT NUMBER

Assign each student a number. Use these to collect papers. You can teach them to sequence. They can line up by their numbers. They can line up by 2's, 5's, 10's, counting, etc. Change the order from time to time.

MIX WORK INTENSITY

Organize the day to provide low intensity activities mixed in between intense academic work times to meet the students' developmental needs of pacing for attention span. A rule-of-thumb is: "A child's attention span is their age plus 10 minutes."

CHECK POINT CHARLIE

Establish a specific time in your daily plans **("Check Point Charlie")** to check students. Review how they are using their time, ask if they have completed certain assignments, and monitor their goals.

STUDENT FILE FOLDERS

Set up student file folders. Students decorate their color-coded folders with die sets or draw their own designs. All of one colored folders go in the Math Box, another color in the Spelling Box, etc. This gives the feeling of ownership and makes more room in their desks. Then at the end of the week or month, the papers can be sent home to parents. Large, plastic, open boxes to store the folders may be purchased at a discount store.

ON-GOING PROJECT FOLDERS

Establish folders for on-going projects which are very important to the individual student. These might include writing, art, research, etc. These are perfect, open-ended assignments to be used when homework is finished.

PRETESTING

Due to the seemingly wider ranges of student abilities, pretesting of units better targets the individual. Do some enrichment with some right away while others do some basic foundation building.

COMPANION READING

Teach reading to the "total class." Companion Reading and Whole Language are two such programs which allow students to feel successful without the pressure of the low, middle, and high groupings.

COOPERATIVE GROUPS

Students select new cooperative learning groups for the next two to three weeks. The criteria might be that they have to have 2 to 3 new people from last time, an equal number of boys and girls, etc. They get a controlled choice.

ABILITY GROUPS

Ability group your students in reading with 2 to 3 other teachers. You may wish to include the reading and learning disabled special area teachers. Fewer, smaller reading groups, with longer class periods will result. The same idea can be applied to math.

PERSONAL CONFERENCES

Have students write in personal journals for ten minutes every day. During this time, schedule one student for a personal conference with you. Discuss specific needs, give extra help, socialize, set goals, joke, talk over problems at home or school, etc.

EXTEND LUNCH

You can extend your lunch period. Your grade level team of teachers can establish a strict study period for 10 minutes right after lunch. One teacher can supervise all 2 to 4 groups. Rotate the duty and even have time to go to the bathroom most days.

TWO FOR THE PRICE OF ONE

If you are pressed for time, try doubling up two activities at once. Read to students while they are on their snack break. Accomplish two things at once. This won't work on a daily basis, but might be a good way to catch up on your schedule occasionally.

"A teacher affects eternity; no one can tell where his influence stops."

Henry B. Adams
1838-1918

NOTES:

"Don't confuse activity with productivity."

--*B. W. Luscher, Jr.*
U.S. Postal Service

ON TASK	Have something for the students to do as soon as they come into the room. This sets a business-like tone and is constructive. Make it part of your lesson plans. Develop folders just for these ideas. Examples might include writing, math puzzle, spelling words to work on, a study period for homework, etc.
WEEK'S SCHEDULE	On the first day of each week, give the students a blank schedule with the special areas, etc. written in. Go over the week's schedule while they write in the rest. Review quickly each morning for changes. Students can plan ahead and be more self-directed.
MATH PROGRESS	Schedule in math facts every Friday. Students keep a chart of progress of mastery. Practice is provided with small booklets for each fact kept in a separate file. Students are self-directed and see the teacher when they feel they are ready to pass the next assessment to go on. Manipulatives, dice games, flash cards, and other station activities should be made available, also. **(See example "A", pp. 106 and 107)**
MATH FLASH CARDS	Make flash cards for math and put them on rings. The students have to go through them with a partner in a specific amount of time. Upon accomplishing the criteria, they check off that set behind their names on a chart.
VARIETY OF ACTIVITIES	Have a listing of a variety of activities to do when students have finished their work. This open-ended "to do" list will mean never hearing "I'm done!" Instead, you will have created an attitude of **"What's next?"** Put the list on the board, or out of sight in the back of their assignment books.
READING LOGS	Attach large manila envelopes to the wall as pockets. Label them A-G, H-K, L-N, and O-Z. Students put **Reading Logs**, etc. in them for easy retrieval without having to look through the whole class pile.
NUMBER VERSUS NAME	Assigning a student number to be put on all paperwork is much easier to check than reading through all the names. It is easier to find a number than a name in your grade book.

COMBINATION CLASS

If you have a combination class with some of last year's students in your classroom again, pair the new students up with the older ones at the beginning of the year. This gives support to the new student, makes it easier to follow directions, and the older students feel important as helpers. Phase out as things smooth out.

RECYCLE INFORMATION

Establish learning centers for students to recycle information using different learning modalities. For example: Math = Hear (headsets), Touch (manipulative), and See (flash cards). Include extension activities to challenge the high potential students. An excellent collection of challenges can be found in Math Games and Puzzles, by R.A. Yawin, Xerox Eduction Publications.

RANDOMLY GROUPING STUDENTS

To randomly group students in 3's or more, write each student's name on a wooden tongue depressor near one end. On the other end, put a colored dot so it is easy to see they are all upside down when you put them into a can. Simply draw out the appropriate number of sticks per game. This eliminates negative feelings of being chosen last, and is very fast.

GETTING-TO-KNOW-YOU ENVIRONMENT

Change the seating arrangement and room arrangement every two weeks. This forces all students to sit by every other student sometime during the year. Also, it creates a new interest and freshness within the classroom environment. If they don't like where they are sitting, they all know it isn't forever, just that two week period.

SOCIOGRAMS

Take a quick sociogram at the same time you gather data for a seating arrangement. Ask the students to write down three students they want to sit next to. Try to give them one of their choices. You will be able to see the social dynamics of the class at the same time you're making out the seating chart.

COMPUTER ASSISTANT

Need help in the computer lab? Hard to get to every question fast enough? Select two students to help other students. These two do not do the assigned work that day. Pick students who know what is going on. Rotate different students each period to be helpers. Another trick is to state, "I will help the person with the quietest hand, first."

**ASKING
FOR HELP**

If someone has a question while you are directing a reading group, teach the students not to interrupt you. They must first try other students before they come to you. Teach this as a routine during the first few weeks of school.

**SELF-DIRECTED
LEARNING**

Don't hold those capable students back. Put them on self-directed learning with a calendar of required and optional work in a certain subject area. Schedule in specific skills, oral work, tests, and independent work. This is a real motivator for the whole class, as it is seen as a reward to make self-choices and independent decisions.

**GROUP
FOLDERS**

Use a pocket file folder for each cooperative learning group. Their names are on the outside. Group materials are inside. It makes it easy to collect assignments.

**SHARING
TEXTBOOKS**

Not enough textbooks to go around? Organize desks into groups of four, with two side-by-side and the other two facing each other. This will give them an easy view of the front of the room while making it easy to share materials. (Heterogeneous grouping is recommended.) This is a natural for the Cooperative Learning Teaching Strategy!

**TEACHING
ORGANIZATION**

On your student supply list in the fall, include a medium sized three-ring notebook, dividers, and three-hole punched, lined paper, Teach lessons in how to organize this excellent tool. It is a life-long student need, right through those college years and beyond.

"The years teach much which the days never know."

Ralph Waldo Emerson

NOTES:

"*We must use time as a tool, not as a couch.*"

John F. Kennedy
1917-1963

REVIEW RESPONSI-BILITIES

Each morning list what has to be done and then elicit help from the students to assign time to each item. As students gain experience in decision making, they learn to better manage their own time and organizational skills. This is a life skill worth developing. It saves you time in planning outside of school, too.

PRE-TEST SPELLING

At the start of the year, give a pre-test for your district's spelling. Top students can go "independent" on their spelling. Pair them up to go at their own rate: study, test, and record. Other students may qualify by getting six 100% tests in a row. Spelling time is set aside each week for this and you only have to work with the smaller group for needed guidance.

INDIVIDUAL CONFERENCES

Schedule an individual conference with each student once a week. You will be surprised by the number of positive spin-offs, and insight into yourself and the students.

TALK TIME

Schedule seven minutes for students just to talk to each other about anything. This relaxes them and they are more ready to attend to the next important task.

TEACH SELF RESPONSIBILITY

Schedule a block of time early in the school year for students to learn to be self-responsible. Teach to this and discuss it so that students know what to do (a variety of activities) whenever they complete their assigned work.

FIRST SUBJECT

Schedule math as the first subject of the day. It is structured and usually has an assignment for them to think about as little blocks of free time open up during the day.

TEACHER DIRECTED TO STUDENT DIRECTED

Start your units being more teacher-directed and then move to more totally student-directed. This time (when students do independent work in small groups, with partners, or individually) is productively used to plan, grade papers, and interact as needed. Give students an outline of the unit for each five days and assignments due, along with an overview of the entire unit.

INDIVIDUAL DIFFERENCES

Teach the introduction of each area to the total group and then split off into different levels of expectation by abilities. Tailor your smaller group's experiences and work load to their capabilities.

MATH CONTRACTS
Put capable students on math contracts. Having top students on self-directed activities allows you to give more individual time to those students who need more guidance. The faster students really appreciate not having to slow down for detailed explanations that they already know.

LEARNING PACKETS FOR OTHERS
Have students make their own learning packets for other students. Any subject will do. Type of information that might be included would be word finds, mazes, pictures, bibliography, written reports, vocabulary, etc.

RESEARCH PROJECT
Develop a research project for students to do over a period of several weeks. Include all language arts requirements: speech, drawing, writing, publishing, research skills, proofreading, rewriting, outlining, notetaking, etc.

RESOLVE PROBLEMS
If two or more classes have a common problem with equipment, or playground space for example, choose one student from each class to meet and come up with a fair plan.

CLASS PARTY
Having a class party? Assign 3 to 4 students to do the total planning of the party. They can get other students involved in sub groups for treats, decorating, games, and clean up. Give them 15 minutes to get organized and the rest of the time is on their own.

PROGRESS FORM
If you have other teachers' students, establish a short check-off form to report progress. This can be used for the other teachers' parent-teacher-child conferences, also. Information might include level, achievement, participation, time management, assignment record, recommendations, etc. **(See example "B", p. 108)**

PEER WORK
Have students work together during independent practice time. They peer coach one-to-one. Stronger students drill math skills with students who have not mastered a concept, for instance.

TEACH INDEPENDENT LEARNING

Teach to independent learning. Have stations at least one day per week so that when students complete their work they have **their** own choice of activities to do.

GROUP RESPONSI- BILITIES

Divide the class into groups based upon days of the week or if you have it, the A,B,C,D,E schedule. These groups are self-directed to know when it is their day to share, when to line up, and other activities the teacher directs.

CLEAN-UP DAY

Try the fresh-start approach. Have a **"Clean-up Day"** to catch up on everything. Pull things together, complete all paper work, tie all the loose strings together, and start all over fresh again the next day.

EQUAL TIME

It is easy for the faster student to get more computer time than the slower student. If you have limited access to equipment like this, make a schedule so that every student gets an equal amount of time, no matter what. This helps self-image and teaches fairness.

SPECIAL AREAS FIRST

Do not arrange **your** teaching schedule until **after** the special areas of art, music, Phy. Ed. etc. are assigned. Slot in your subjects so that students do not miss blocks of reading, math, spelling, writing, etc.

SMALL GROUP WORK

Schedule half classes from two different classes to go to Phy. Ed. at the same time. This leaves you without a break, but you gain working with only one half of your class. It is much easier to group for reading/math/etc. when you can plan on only having half as many students for an hour (two Phy. Ed. classes in a row). Do you have a grade level team teacher that will agree?

GYM SHOES

Gym shoes are easily stored in pop cases tipped on end. A 24-sized case will hold 12 pair of shoes. Print student names on the outside end of the boxes.

NOTES:

"To save time, you must be well prepared, not only what you teach (lesson plans), but with supplies, materials, and transition activities."

--Florence Swenson

NAME_____

**Fill in the blanks when

$$2$$

is the factor:

SCORE_____ +/11 plus 2 E.C.

X0		X7	
X1		X8	
X2		X9	
X3		X10	
X4		X11	
X5		X12	
X6			

NAME_____

**Fill in the blanks when

$$3$$

is the factor:

SCORE_____ +/11 plus 2 E.C.

X0		X7	
X1		X8	
X2		X9	
X3		X10	
X4		X11	
X5		X12	
X6			

READING GROUP SUMMARY

NAME _____   READING TEACHER _____

                                            DATE _____

1. SRA IIB   READING LAB. HAS COMPLETED _____ LEVELS.
      (MUST READ 10 SELECTIONS PER COLOR)

2. READING LOG SHOWS _____ ENTRIES COMPLETED.

3. MOST RECENT UNIT TEST SCORE SHOWS   **M   P   S**

4. PRESENT READING LEVEL IS _____ UNIT _____

5. ACHIEVEMENT LEVEL OF TASKS:

                        SKILLPAC PAGES **M   P   S**

                        FOCUS QUESTIONS **M   P   S**

6. ORAL READING SKILL (PREVIOUS READING) **M   P   S**

7. SMALL GROUP PARTICIPATION   **ACTIVE   USUALLY   SELDOM**
      (TASK DISCUSSIONS)

8. TIME MANAGEMENT   **EXCELLENT GOOD   NEEDS ADJUSTMENT**

9. RECOMMENDATIONS:

NOTES:

"We should all be concerned about the future because we will have to spend the rest of our lives there."

C. F. Kettering
1876-1958

Chapter VIII - New Students

INTRODUCTION

A new student arriving after the school year has started always poses a break in your routine.

This chapter relates to assessing needs, preparing your class, and catching the new student up on background work, routine, expectations, physical setting, and requirements.

Give the new students plenty of support to decrease their anxiety. If **you** are prepared, your anxiety, as well as theirs, will be lessened.

NOTES:

"Those who are happy do not observe how time goes by."

Proverbs

NEW STUDENT FOLDER

Develop a new student folder. Just pull it out when a new student arrives at your classroom. Material and information that you want to use is thought of when you have time rather than during the bustle of the day. Include material that went home to your regular students at the beginning of the year, school rules and procedures, blank name tags, a class list, a class schedule, locker number, class picture with names, and a checklist of where to add the student's name (charts, grade book, bulletin board lists, parent folders, report card, progress sheets, emergency card, etc.). Don't forget a list of procedures to do such as introduce to other teachers, tour of the school, contact the parents, assign a buddy for the day, get a desk and chair, tour of the room, etc.

PREPARING THE CLASS

Start preparing the class before you ever get a new student. Discuss what it would be like to come to this classroom for someone new. Discuss prior experiences they have had. Set the stage for acceptance and feelings.

PARENT/ GUARDIAN MEETING

Try to meet with the parent(s)/guardian(s) prior to the student's arrival. Gather information about the student and their relationship to their family and school. Check parent's perceptions of their child and how the child feels about him/herself. This gives you a basis on which to make better decisions about arrangements in the classroom to make it more comfortable.

INTRODUCTIONS

Ask the new student how he/she would like to be introduced and any information that he/she would like to have shared. Assign another student to be his/her "buddy" for the day to answer questions and show around.

GETTING TO KNOW YOU

Have all students, including the new one, write on **"Getting to Know You."** Let the new student take this collection home after it has been shared orally. Include hobbies, likes, dislikes, things about your room, etc. Write one, yourself. The new parents will enjoy this special language arts activity, too.

LUNCH

Eat lunch with the new student. It sets a tone of caring, rapport, and you will get to know them quicker in this more informal setting.

ROUTE CHECK   Make sure they get onto the correct bus or to their parent's car, or on the right street at the end of the day. Walk with them until you see them on the right track.

CHECK THE RECORDS   Follow up on records coming from the previous school. Check reading level, health problems, and family data right away. Read thoroughly as soon as possible.

"We can scarcely hate anyone that we know."

William Hazlitt